THE INDOOR CAT

The Indoor Cat

How to Understand, Enjoy, and Care for House Cats

PATRICIA CURTIS

Foreword by Audrey A. Hayes, V.M.D.

D O U B L E D A Y & C O M P A N Y , I N C.
G A R D E N   C I T Y ,   N E W   Y O R K   1 9 8 1

Cover photo by Mary Bloom
Endpapers photo by Walter Chandoha

ISBN: 0-385-15368-6
Library of Congress Catalog Card Number: 79-6578

Copyright © 1981 by Patricia Curtis

To my dog, Dandelion,
a friend to cats

Acknowledgments

My special thanks go to Dr. Audrey Hayes, who served as my consultant and expert reader. I was fortunate indeed to be able to rely on Audrey's commitment to cats, her expertise and experience as a veterinarian, and the careful guidance she gave me in every chapter.

I also wish to thank Cathleen Jordan, my editor. What luck to have an editor who also loves cats. Her suggestions and support helped me greatly.

I owe much to my cat-owning friends whose anecdotes enrich these pages. Thank you, all of you.

And a round of catnip to the many cats I have known, to whom I am everlastingly grateful for teaching me so much about themselves.

—Patricia Curtis

Contents

Foreword by Audrey A. Hayes, V.M.D.   xiii

chapter one
The Indoor Cat: What's Different About It   1
Do indoor cats suffer? Confinement stress. Your
captive tiger. The overrated outdoors.

chapter two
How Many: One Cat or Two or More   10
The single-kitten mistake. Take two. Three or more.
Male or female? Choosing a cat. Where to get a cat.

chapter three
Kitten, Adolescent, and Adult: How to Mix and Match   24
Introductions. Kittens. And adolescents. Adult cats.
Cautions.

chapter four
Diet: For the Lounge Lizard or the Gymnast   34
How much food how often. Water. What to feed.
Gourmets. The vegetarian cat. Feeding bowls.
Feeding problems.

chapter five
Routine Upkeep: Hygiene and Grooming   49
The litter box. Litter-box training. Your cat's coat.
Bathing a cat. Your cat's nails. Ear grooming. Care
of the teeth.

chapter six

Safety: The High-rise Syndrome and
Other Hazards   63
> The high-rise syndrome. Poisoning. House plants.
> Swallowed foreign objects. Heat stroke. Burns.
> Hiding places.

chapter seven

General Health: Illnesses, Vaccinations,
Neutering   80
> Symptoms of illness. Vaccinations. Urolithiasis. Fe-
> line leukemia and other cancers. Internal parasites
> (worms). External parasites. Ringworm. Allergies.
> Diarrhea and constipation. Hair balls. Heart dis-
> ease. Between owner and pet. How to administer
> medicine. How to take a cat's temperature. Patient
> care. Neutering.

chapter eight

Behavior Problems and Bad Habits: How to
Avoid or Cure Them   108
> Breaking litter-box training. Scratching furniture.
> Declawing. Eating house plants. Nursing. Crying.
> Aggressiveness. Scolding a cat.

chapter nine

Communication and Play: Keeping Your Cat
Happy and Loving   127
> Conversing with your cat. Cat body language.
> Games cats play. Toys for a cat. Sitting and sleep-
> ing places. The sociable, affectionate cat.

appendix

   Miscellaneous Information for

   Indoor Cat Owners   146
        The cat and babies and children. The cat and the
        dog. Traveling with a cat. Leaving a cat home
        when you travel. The geriatric cat. Euthanizing a
        cat. Providing for your cat if you die.

Index   166

Foreword

Some people become veterinarians because they had pets as children and became deeply interested in animals from this early association. When I was a child, I never had any pets—only a large collection of stuffed animals. They were an unsatisfactory substitute for the real thing.

When I grew up, I joined the Ringling Brothers Barnum & Bailey Circus for a while. I was an aerialist and an elephant rider, but I especially liked the big cats. I learned a lot about those marvelous performing animals.

I had no cat of my own, however, until I was an undergraduate at Hunter College, in New York. My husband and I adopted a stray kitten that became our first indoor cat. That was fourteen years ago, and we still have him. Other cats have joined our household, but T.C., by his own assumption and everyone else's concession, is very much Top Cat.

Another of our cats, G.G., was acquired when I was in veterinary school. She had been purchased from an animal dealer for student surgery, and had already been spayed and declawed by one of the other veterinary students. The plan called for this student to perform another operation on her and then euthanize her. He was reluctant to do this. She was a pretty cat and he had grown fond of her but couldn't keep her. He mentioned his feelings to me.

I went to her cage and looked at her, and she looked out at me. I already had T.C. and two other cats at home, so I wasn't really in the market for another. But why couldn't I take her, I thought, and then find a good home for her? After all, a nice gray cat that has already been spayed and declawed—surely someone would want her. So I just sort of spirited her out of the laboratory.

What I hadn't realized was that while G.G. was in good health physically, the emotional damage she had suffered somewhere in her past was great. G.G. apparently had never forgiven that first human being, whoever it was, that had abused or abandoned her and caused her to wind up in a dealer's and then in a laboratory. So while G.G. was friendly enough toward my other cats, she was terrified of people.

When prospective adopters came to my house to see her, we had to search for her and drag her out from the back of a closet or under the bed. Naturally this turned off people who might otherwise have given her a good home. (And it inspired my husband to name her G.G.—Gray Ghost—because we rarely saw her.)

Finally I decided that she would have to be my cat, and that was that. And I have never regretted my decision to keep her, since in winning the trust of this timid cat I have learned many valuable lessons about handling and treating the frightened cats presented to me by their owners for veterinary care.

I learn things daily from my own cats that are useful to me in my practice. And just recently G.G. gave me one of the most valuable insights into the nature of cats that I have ever had. It came about through an illness she developed. I didn't have to be a veterinarian to see that she was going to the litter box more frequently, passing small amounts of bloody urine, eating a little less, drinking a little more water. I put G.G. in her carrier and brought her to the animal hospital where I work. The results of her X rays and blood tests indicated that she needed an operation to relieve a blockage.

Believe me, G.G. got the best of everything. She came

through the operation with no medical or surgical complications, and I visited her several times during my workdays. Wouldn't you think a normal cat in these circumstances would make a good recovery? Not G.G.—she went downhill rapidly. She wouldn't eat; she lost nearly 25 percent of her weight. She became depressed and listless. A long weekend was approaching, and I realized that if I left her in the hospital, she would decide she had no reason to go on living.

So I took her home and devoted three days completely to her. I had to coax her to eat every mouthful. I bought her roast beef and followed her around, hand-feeding her. I held her for hours. It was five days before I was even sure G.G. would live. Finally, after about a week, she was convinced I really cared about her, and she wanted to get well.

There comes a time in the course of every animal's illness when to keep the animal in the hospital is merely running up the bill. If everything being done for the pet in the hospital can be done by the owner at home, the animal is better off there. When a cat is sick or injured, it should not be treated as if it were a car that has broken down and is in need of repairs. It is not always possible to fix whatever was wrong with it and return to the owner a perfectly functioning machine.

The recovery chances of every sick or injured cat depend on three potentials: the cat's will to live, the owner's involvement with the cat, and the veterinarian's skill. As veterinarians, we strive for the owner's cooperation, because without it, the animal has a poor chance.

I can't say it too often—the most important quality a cat owner can develop is the understanding of each cat's unique personality and the awareness of any change in each cat's normal behavior. After all, the owner, especially the owner of an indoor cat, has a far greater opportunity to know the animal better than we do. My objective in helping with the preparation of this book is to assist cat owners to become more observant of their pets, understand them, and take good care of them—to the mutual benefit of both the cats and their owners.

Whenever I am seeing patients in the course of my work, I automatically try to remember that to the owner, his or her cat is the ONLY cat in the hospital. I may have seen forty cats that same day before this one, but I know that at that moment, this is the only cat that counts. Some veterinarians may not understand how pet owners feel until they have been in their shoes with a sick animal that they love.

I think people who don't have pets, cats especially, are missing a lot. It has always been my belief that there are no people who really don't like cats—only people who don't know cats.

Audrey A. Hayes, V.M.D.
DIPLOMATE, AMERICAN COLLEGE
OF VETERINARY INTERNAL
MEDICINE
ASSOCIATE STAFF VETERINARIAN,
DEPARTMENT OF MEDICINE,
THE ANIMAL MEDICAL CENTER,
NEW YORK, N.Y.

THE INDOOR CAT

chapter one

The Indoor Cat:

What's Different About It

It has been said the domestic cat was invented to give human beings the pleasure of caressing the tiger.

While I reject this adage out-of-hand because of its anthropocentric assumption that any species of animal was "invented" for the use of human beings, it is nevertheless certainly fun to stroke the small tigerlike animal that is the domestic cat. The cat has lived with people for several thousand years. It seems unlikely that it willingly cast its lot with us, back in the beginning. If it did, it has certainly had much cause to regret it, considering the abuse this often maligned and misunderstood creature has suffered at our hands. While all animals have been tyrannized by people, the domestic cat has inspired the most bizarre forms of torture.

Still, in a few human societies the cat has enjoyed respect and affection among people with sense enough to appreciate its unique ways. And the cat, given half a chance, makes a devoted pet for people who befriend it.

Up until the recent past, a cat made its owner's house its home base but had its own private life outdoors—in the barnyard, the neighborhood, the backyard. The cat was more often than not a working member of the household, keeping the mice and rats at zero population growth.

With the urbanization of American life, more and more people moved to the cities, often to apartment houses, and brought cats with them. But for the cats, the city has turned out to be full of hazards. Outdoors, they get lost in a maze of buildings, they get run over by cars. They fall or jump out of windows, get trapped in basements, are stolen by strangers, and catch diseases from one another.

So it has become the practice of city and suburban people to protect their cats by keeping them confined indoors. And thanks to its wonderful adaptability and strong survival instincts, the cat has become the ideal indoor pet.

Do indoor cats suffer?

Many cat owners feel pangs of guilt about keeping their pets indoors. In fact, some city dwellers—especially those in apartments—refuse to keep cats because they think it would be cruel to confine them.

Sure, ideally, cats should have access to both the cozy indoors *and*, if not the open countryside, at least to protected outdoor areas. But the time has passed when they can safely roam, even in most rural areas. Domestic cats, being totally dependent on people, have to live where we are. And all but a small percentage of us—in the United States, at least—live in cities or towns. So, realistically, the time is gone when we can debate about where cats should live. The cats are *here*, now, and they need us even more than we need them.

Cats do not necessarily suffer from confinement. In fact, a major difference of indoor cats is that they enjoy longer and healthier lives than their counterparts on the street, in the yard, or on the farm. Many of the reservations people have about keeping cats indoors may stem from mistaken notions about the nature of cats. If you believe that cats are aloof, independent, unaffectionate, self-sufficient creatures who have to go their own way to be happy, then you will view confining a cat with the same repugnance as if it were in a prison. Seems to me that Rudyard Kipling did the world's cats a disservice when he wrote his famous story about the cat that walked by himself, to whom all places were alike. Cats aren't that way at all.

Because cats will defend themselves when molested, because they are somewhat subtle in displaying their affections, because they are not easily cowed and have, I believe, a high degree of self-respect, they have an undeserved reputation for vanity, arrogance, and indifference. They are also falsely believed to have some almost mystical ability to get along on their own (a notion any animal-welfare activist can document otherwise with staggering figures).

Observations of the house cat's wild relatives should reassure owners about keeping their pets indoors: distance running is not their nature. All the wild cats, large or small, hunt by stalking, ambushing, pouncing, and perhaps by short sprints. They are not coursing animals, like dogs. So while your dog may need frequent chances to run farther than the distance from one room to the next, your cat does not.

Also, wild cats—and there's no evidence that the ancestor of the modern domestic cat was any different—spend most of their time sleeping or resting. Lions in their natural state, for example, are known to lie around—sleeping, dozing, or just gazing—sixteen to twenty hours a day. If your pet cat does the same, it doesn't mean it simply has nothing else to do indoors; it is behaving normally.

If you know something about cats and understand their

true needs, and if you are sensitive to your own particular cat, you can give it an indoor life that is rich and happy as well as comfortable, healthy, and safe.

Confinement stress

This is not to say that confinement can create no problems at all. The indoor cat of an uninformed and negligent owner may be neurotic, extremely unhappy, and in poor health. Some owners have unrealistic expectations of their cats; some are just indifferent.

It is known that among zoo animals, most of which are born in captivity, confinement is a powerful stress factor. Indeed, boredom is a leading cause of sickness among zoo animals. They develop illnesses and exhibit neurotic behavior patterns and abnormal habits—head shaking, rocking, continual pacing or walking the bars of their cages, apathy, licking parts of their bodies raw, refusal to mate, infanticide—all symptoms of stress. Malnutrition from lack of appetite, or obesity from overeating, is also a boredom factor that zoo personnel recognize all too often among the animals in their care.

A domestic cat confined to a house or apartment will, in certain circumstances, develop stress symptoms of its own, lead a joyless life, and give its owner little pleasure.

Modern zoo scientists and animal ethologists have become aware that the stress of confinement can be eliminated or greatly reduced by providing captive animals with the right type of environment. Space to move about freely is important, but even more so is the complexity of the confinement area. Actual size of a cage, for example, is not as important as the opportunities the cage affords an animal to perform some of its natural functions.

Depending on the type of animal, of course, if it is confined with vines to swing on, trees to climb, a pool to swim in, or a place to dig—if it can play, sun itself, and above all, *hide*—a zoo animal will suffer comparatively little from the stress of captivity, certainly not anywhere near the extent of some poor creature in a bare, concrete cage in continual view of the public. Similarly, zoo animals that live in pairs or groups are known to do better than solitary animals. Like most human beings, most animals are social to some degree, large or small.

Today, better zoos are attempting to compromise between their budgets and the whims of the public on the one hand and the actual needs of the animals on the other. They are belatedly trying to improve the lives of captive animals by designing better habitats for them. In a new and well-planned zoo in the Panaewa rain forest in Hawaii, for example, tigers live together in an artificial jungle, secluded, for the most part, from the public and provided with mechanical "game" to stalk and chase. In short, they are able to lead a good approximation of normal lives. Think about that the next time you see a solitary, arthritic animal lying stupefied with defeat and boredom in the small, bare, concrete cage that is the home of most zoo tigers.

Your captive tiger

Is the comparison to zoo animals far-fetched when talking about an animal such as the house cat, which has not been wild for dozens of centuries? Not at all, in terms of the effects of confinement.

A cat with access to the outdoors can explore, socialize, climb, sharpen its claws, chase, and hide. It can bury its wastes in a fresh spot every time. It's true that a cat who can do all this safely and *also* be fed regularly, come indoors for warmth and human companionship, and sleep on its owner's bed is living in the best of all possible worlds. But as you may have noticed, few of us—and few other animals—live in a perfect world. That being the case, the best thing for a cat and its city- or suburban-dwelling owner is a life-style that provides opportunities for the animal to still do most of those normal cat activities—indoors. Given these approximations, the cat will adapt without turning a whisker. A cat that's given plenty of freedom in a house or apartment, a window to look out, some hiding places, toys, and an interested and caring owner has a complex enough environment.

The owners of indoor cats have much to gain from the pet's captive situation: your cat is visible for you to observe, it's there for you to enjoy its interesting and delightful ways. Instead of the animal gracefully chasing a butterfly in the garden by itself, it can be pirouetting with a toy right in your living room. Cats are endlessly wonderful and amusing to watch. Owners of indoor cats have the advantage of being more likely to catch their animals being themselves; you're less apt to miss that cute position, that phenomenally intelligent act, that remarkable leap.

But because of its comparatively sedentary life, the indoor cat requires a somewhat different diet than that of a cat who can roam. It doesn't need a layer of fat to keep its body warm. Too many indoor cats are just plain fat. Because it can't seek companionship for itself, it needs company provided for it—you and other people, other animals. It needs opportunity for exercise, sometimes encouraged by you in the form of play. It requires specific protections, such as screens in open windows so it won't fall out, closed doors so it can't wander out and get hurt or lost. And this superb predator needs the kind of toys that satisfy its instinct to hunt and pounce—toys such as wine corks that the cat can pretend are beetles or field mice, a wad of paper that rustles like a leaf, a large paper bag that becomes a lair.

The indoor cat may present an unwary owner with problems that stem from its situation. It may tend to chew up house plants when it craves grass, sharpen its claws on furniture for lack of tree bark, and climb the draperies or leap to the top shelf of a cabinet of breakable treasures to achieve the lofty vantage point cats enjoy. All of these traits can be dealt with successfully, to the satisfaction of both of you.

Interestingly enough, a cat that has never been outdoors, or one who has forgotten what it was like, may be terrified if it is suddenly taken out. In the past, yielding to the mistaken notion that I was doing my indoor cats a big favor, I have taken them for supervised walks outdoors when opportunities presented themselves during weekends or summers spent out of the city. All the cats were extremely uncomfortable. They flattened themselves out to what looked like three feet long and three inches high and skulked fearfully along on their bellies. In time, I suppose, these agoraphobes could have been induced to enjoy the outdoors, but it seemed unfair to put them through this discomfort for only temporary freedom.

Some fortunate cats live with people who regularly take them on weekends or vacations to places where they can wander outdoors a bit if they wish. Cats, being the flexible creatures they are, soon adjust to these situations once they become familiar. They learn to enjoy the freedom of the lawn or garden and then return to their city homes with perfect poise. A cat should be protected, however, from such dangers as roads, cat-hating dogs, traps, farm vehicles, and other hazards of country life. A basically city cat especially should be supervised when it's on the loose, and never allowed to stay out all night.

Occasionally you'll meet or read about a cat that walks on a leash and goes about with its owner just like a dog. These anomalies were invariably raised to this life as very young kittens and seem none the worse for it.

The overrated outdoors

One summer I took my two indoor cats with us to a suburban house with a large yard on a quiet street where we lived for a month. They were never happy when we took them outdoors. They preferred to lie in the screened windows and gaze out.

We even had a disaster with one of them, a beloved calico named Becky who belonged to my young daughter. On an expedition to the back lawn, Becky suddenly was frightened by something, fled up a tall tree, and was afraid to come down. The branches were too high for us to reach, even with a long ladder. We coaxed and offered food, to no avail. Neighbors advised that when night came, or when she got hungry enough, Becky would figure out a way to get down. I had no confidence in this opinion. Becky stayed in the tree all night, crying, as my daughter lay in her bed, also crying. Next day was the same. I appealed to a local humane society in vain—they said their contract with the community was only to rescue dogs. I didn't even bother to call the fire department, because there was no way the truck with its ladders could have driven near enough to the tree.

Finally, the second evening I went into the town's police station for advice. There, a kindly sheriff, an experienced cat person himself, called up just the right professional to rescue our Becky—a tree surgeon. The man arrived soon at our house, put on his tree-climbing gear, and up he went. He carried a large bag over his shoulder to put Becky in when he reached her, but it turned out to be unnecessary. When he came close enough, she climbed gratefully down onto his shoulder and balanced there as he descended.

Becky never ventured outdoors again during our stay in the suburban house. She opted for staying in, even when offered an open door. So much for the highly touted freedom of the great outdoors, as far as this indoor cat was concerned.

I once lived in a garden apartment where my cats could go in and out as they pleased, not to the street but to the intriguing gardens of the entire inside of a city block. But the time came when I was getting ready to move, with them, to a smaller third-floor apartment where they would become totally indoor cats. I felt bad that they would be deprived of the ideal lives they now led. One gorgeous spring day when the garden door was open, the air humming with birdsongs and the sunshine dappling the flagstones in the yard, I happened to pass through the living room and noticed something interesting. Every one of my free-to-go-out cats was sacked out on the sofa, snoring peacefully. Were they really going to miss the outdoors so much?

Bear in mind that the domestic cat, indoors or out or both, normally spends most of its time (1) sleeping, (2) sitting, and (3) grooming itself, anyway. So you are not depriving it of these important pastimes by keeping it indoors. The other activities—hunting, playing, watching, hiding, for instance—require a little effort from you. The purpose of this book is to help you identify the needs of your captive cat and to suggest ways to provide for them. I hope to help you get the most pleasure from your pet and give it the best possible indoor life.

chapter two

How Many:
One Cat or Two or More

For a few seconds, I couldn't figure out what had awakened me—it was the middle of the night. Then I heard the sounds in the living room—scampering and rattling, objects falling to the floor, papers rustling, little musical chirps. I looked at the illuminated face of my bedside clock: four-thirty. I looked at my three cats at the foot of my bed, crouched comfortably on their stomachs, front paws tucked under their chests, riding the blankets like ducks on a pond. They were staring toward the bedroom door that opened into the living room. Even in the darkness, I could interpret their posture and facial expressions as utter disbelief. They had been appalled enough when the young cat had joined our household yesterday morning. Now we were all appalled.

This four-month-old juvenile delinquent was to be our guest for a week while his owner was out of town. The permanent residents in my apartment were the three adult cats, one middle-aged dog, and me. The visitor had seemed cautious about the dog, and he had ignored me, but already he had pestered Gina, Olivia, and Fred relentlessly.

Worst of all, I had gotten us all into this situation.

The single-kitten mistake

In my heart, I know that everyone who doesn't have a cat is not necessarily leading a deprived life, just as I know, intellectually at least, that people who dislike cats are not automatically bad people. But once in a while I make friends with a catless person who seems to be perfect for a cat, an obviously potential cat lover who needs only a little help to blossom into the real thing.

Recently I had become acquainted with just such a person—a young woman living alone in a quite large apartment who had seemed taken with my cats. She would sit on my sofa petting Gina and remarking what a delightful animal she was. Whenever I suggested she get a cat of her own, she seemed uncertain but at the same time not opposed to the idea.

And so it came to pass that when I saw a sign on a door in my neighborhood: "Yellow kitten for adoption" . . . well, here he was, some months later, chasing imaginary mice in my living room when he and the rest of us should have been fast asleep.

My friend had been extremely nervous about taking on this animal. She had never had a pet in her life. She liked to be footloose; the responsibility might impair her mobility, she ventured. Suppose she turned out to be allergic? Dubiously, she eyed the little yellow ball that fit in the pocket of my skirt.

If you had gone to Central Casting and asked for a kitten, a perfect kitten that embodied all that a kitten is supposed to be, you would have been handed this one. Here was the quintessential kitten: cute, healthy, pretty, bright-eyed,

lively, curious, outgoing, cuddly—the works. My friend
wasn't even sure how to hold him. We all demonstrated.
Looking a bit wild-eyed, she took him home, along with a
book on cat care which I lent her. She went out and bought
cat food, a litter box, a china bowl with "kitty" in blue let-
ters on the side, a catnip mouse.

For the better part of a week, I got several phone calls a
day. "He just sneezed—is he sick?" "What does it mean
when he hides his catnip mouse in my bedroom slipper?"
"How do I teach him not to jump up and eat out of my
plate when I'm having dinner?" "I can't find him—he's been
missing for an hour!"

Then things seemed to settle down a bit. My friend
named her pet Pushkin and took him to the vet for his shots.
She bought him all sorts of toys and an upholstered climb-
ing post. I felt satisfied that I had not only enriched my
friend's life but provided a little animal with a good home.

After about four weeks, however, I began to notice many
scratches on the young woman's hands and arms. "He flat-
tens his ears back and charges at me," she explained. "Sometimes he holds my arm and bites and kicks with his hind
feet. It wasn't so bad when he was tiny. Now he hurts."

She began to mention treasured objects he had broken,
plants he had eaten. She spent many hours playing with him
whenever she could, she said, but he was inexhaustible. She
was puzzled and not pleased by many of his habits. She
came down with a severe case of mixed feelings. Pushkin
seemed to pick up her doubts about him and became increasingly highstrung.

I had to examine my lapse of good judgment. Here was a
person with an exquisite apartment and a busy life—she
went to work five days a week and often was out in the evening also. Here was a normal, lively, social animal who
found himself alone for as many as twenty out of twenty-
four hours a day, because also she shut him out of her bed-

room at night. She had to because he disturbed her by romping over her or tearing noisily around the room.

His day began when she came home from work. He would gobble his dinner and be ready for play. But if she went out for the evening, he had nothing to do again—and again, no human voice or footfall. He couldn't go out and seek his own diversions and companionship. Since she lived on the twenty-sixth floor, he couldn't even see anything to watch out the windows.

I visited my friend and her pet. The little cat sat on her lap at every opportunity, followed her from room to room. He seemed to love her. The attacks on her arms and legs were probably meant in play, I decided, unless he somehow sensed her lack of commitment to him and in his anxiety was punishing her. The sad fact was that she was getting very little of the pleasure of having a cat, in proportion to the problems.

I should have known better. A single kitten is not the best pet for a person who lives alone and is out a great deal. I should have sold my friend on the idea of acquiring an older, settled cat—or better yet, two kittens. A pair of kittens are not only company for each other but expend a lot of their energy on one another. They are good wrestling mates, reducing much of the wear and tear on the owner's arms and legs. Pushkin would have been a far easier cat to live with if he'd had a sibling or friend all along.

It's true that some people take single kittens and raise them with relatively few problems into normal, happy indoor cats. I believe they are exceptions.

Take two

As a general rule, it is not a good idea to keep a cat of any age as the only pet if it is to live indoors and the people in the household are out much of the time. Folks have the mistaken notion that cats are aloof and independent, and that they can stay alone most of the time, or for long periods, without becoming lonely. While cats are perhaps not as dependent as dogs on human companionship, they do need us greatly. For a single indoor cat, you're *it*—the whole world—and your presence is as essential as food and water.

I had always thought that my cat Fred, who has never been outwardly fond of other cats in our household but who certainly loves me inordinately, would like to be the Only Cat. He always seemed to say, "When you've got me, what do you need these other cats for?" He was middle-aged, ten, when we moved out of the garden duplex. For a few months I stayed with a friend while waiting to move into my next apartment, and I distributed four of the cats temporarily with my now-grown children and kept Fred at the friend's with me. I thought, at last things are the way Fred would like them—he has me all to himself. But clearly, Fred was lonely. Whenever I would come home, he seemed pitifully glad to see me and would cling to me, partly perhaps from being in a strange home, but mainly I think because he missed the other cats.

At first thought, it might seem that two cats would be twice as much trouble as one. But in some ways, they are less trouble. For one thing, if you have at least two, you have greater freedom to be away from home. The knowledge that there are two to keep each other company when you're out can be a relief. A lonely pet anxiously awaiting your return can be a troubling thought in the back of your mind when you've been gone many hours. It is cruel to leave a single cat alone over a weekend, even if someone looks in on it and feeds it. But so long as someone comes in daily to tend to their needs, two or more cats can spend even a few weeks alone in each other's company without undue stress.

N.B. For information on the subject of leaving your pet or pets when you go away, see Index.

A person adopting a cat who *must* be the Only Cat will find that, unlike a kitten, a well socialized older cat is best. Such a cat can be found at a good humane shelter or obtained from a private individual who for one reason or another has to give up a pet (see *Where to get a cat*, below). The fact that someone is putting a cat up for adoption doesn't necessarily mean that there's anything wrong with it.

If you can't have two cats, you might consider another animal. There are many instances of cat-and-dog friendships, and even a well-protected bird or hamster is better than nothing. A goldfish or other tropical fish in an aquarium, while certainly interesting for a cat to watch, does not really qualify as a companion to a cat.

Three or more

Many years ago when we first moved into the ground-floor duplex apartment of the quaint two-family house with a garden, we had two cats, Fred and Becky. Within a few days we found a yellow cat starving out back and began to feed him. He was so weak from hunger that he could only walk a few steps and then lie down. A few days later, when the poor animal made a heroic effort to climb in our kitchen window, we decided he was our cat, and he stayed. My daughter named him Baxter.

Before long I adopted an irresistible gray-and-white tabby kitten—Gina—from a neighborhood cat shelter. Then a huge, black, sick, and bad-tempered cat was forced on us who, after being isolated, nursed back to health, castrated, and reassured, became our jolly and affectionate Eldridge. That made five indoor-outdoor cats, and some people concluded that I had crossed over the line that separates the simple cat lover from the hard-core eccentric.

But my cats were neutered, healthy, clean, friendly, and home-loving. I brushed them to keep the flying cat hairs under control, and although the cats went outdoors to the yard at will, I kept two clean litter boxes in the apartment— one upstairs and one down.

Perhaps because they could go out when they wished to get away from one another, there was never any contre-temps among them when stray or visiting cats dined with them. But one summer, a curious thing happened. A hungry cat turned up and, after establishing that he was homeless and having him checked out by our veterinarian, I took him in too. Although he was no troublemaker, the five cats didn't like him a bit. They quarreled with him and began to fight with each other. Suddenly all the cats seemed irritable and unhappy. It dawned on me that they were trying to tell me something. The ecological limit of our household, as far as the cats were concerned, had been exceeded. Quickly, I managed to find a good home for the new cat, and peace once more returned.

On the other hand, just the opposite can happen. Once, my son and his girlfriend had three resident cats—Thompson Jones, Carla, and Clarence—who were not particularly fond of each other or compatible. Thompson is shy and passive, Carla is crotchety, and Clarence is a pest. Then Fidel, a lively young neutered male, moved in. Fidel is yellow and has the build of a Boston Globe Trotter—long, slim, and muscular. Fidel can't believe that anyone doesn't love him. When any one of the three cats snarled at him, shunned, or even swatted him, he would respond by pinning the other cat to the floor and washing it. His soothing tongue would quiet the attacker until it had no anger left. A cat apparently can't stay mad when it's being gently licked. Gradually the older cats not only came to like Fidel, they stopped fighting among themselves and became friends. Fidel established harmony in the household.

I don't think there is any hard rule about how many cats should live in a house or apartment of whatever size. There are too many variables. In addition to the number and size of the rooms, and the number of cats the family is comfortable with, there are such factors as the sizes and ages of the cats, their temperaments, and their relationships with each other. Some people live in a spacious apartment with two cats and that's plenty for them. But I have friends who keep twenty-two cats harmoniously and hygienically in a large house and wouldn't part with any of them.

Male or female?

"Male cats prefer women and female cats like men"—how often have I heard that? It's true my cinnamon tabby Olivia seems to have a definite liking for men and is often overly familiar toward them. She tends to jump, invited or not, into the laps of male visitors before she'll choose a female lap. But in general, I don't believe that cats are particularly aware of the sexes of people. They do respond best to well-modulated human voices, they will certainly choose a light human footstep over a heavy one, and they do tend to shy away from people who are given to making sudden sweeping gestures and gross movements. But these traits can be present in men or women.

Possibly male kittens are more active than females, and male cats do tend to grow somewhat larger than females. But since your indoor cat, for its own sake and yours, will of course be neutered (see Chapter Seven), it will tend to be somewhat androgynous and its sexual characteristics will be modified anyway.

Whether you choose two or more males, two or more females, or one or several of each doesn't matter in the least in terms of their friendships with each other. Siblings generally do love each other for life when raised together and kept together. But cats can become fast friends for the same reasons we do—simply because they like one another's personality.

And some cats may never become particularly good friends but still get something from each other's company— like Fred, who I thought wanted nothing more than to be the Only Cat but who turned out to miss his housemates. Even cats that flatly dislike each other still are better off together, unless one is terrorizing the other. Simply watching one another with distaste gives them something to do.

Choosing a cat

There's one theory that a kitten that has been only with its mother and siblings and had little contact with human beings in its early life will always be shy and withdrawn around people. Maybe so, in general. But my Fred was born in a greenhouse and hidden by his mother, never touched by human beings until one day, when he was about eight weeks old, he was captured, put in a box, brought on a train and subway, and placed on my desk in an office. When I first laid eyes on him, he was out of his mind with fear. He spent his first week in my house under a dresser. He was a perfect example of this theory. But now, while he has always been easily spooked by sudden noises and heavy footsteps, if affection were measured on a scale of one to ten, Fred would rate an eleven. Not just with me, but with visitors too. So in choosing a kitten or young cat, don't be turned off by a shy one.

Some people, in selecting an animal in a pound or pet shop, or inspecting one brought to their home, only want an animal that responds to them at first sight. They expect the cat to take one look at them, leap into their arms, and put its paws around their neck. A cat that shrinks away from them or seems distracted hasn't got a chance. These folks usually make wonderful owners for the animal that by pure chance happens to warm up immediately to them—but they haven't got a clue to the true nature of cats. A cat may be so frightened, confused, or curious in a strange or upsetting place that it simply isn't capable of relating well to a new human being at that moment. If you have too rigid an expectation of the cat, and don't take into consideration what *it* may be feeling when you meet it, you might pass up a superb pet. By those standards, Fred would never have been adopted.

I don't mean to imply that all cats make equally good pets, or that you can take in any cat of any age and temperament and, with proper treatment and enough affection, turn it into a loving pet. Some cats just never become well socialized, even if you do everything right. An awful lot does depend on its earliest experiences with human beings, on what it learned from its mother, and I suppose even on its heredity. But in all my experiences with many, many cats, I have come to believe that unless it has been tormented and brutalized, or lived too long without human contact, almost any cat can become a rewarding pet for someone who really likes cats.

There are cat owners who adore their own pets without necessarily being hard-core, card-carrying cat lovers. Others —and I am of this type—not only love our own cats in particular but cats in general. I guess you could say we also simply like the *essence* of cats, what you might call cat-ness.

In adopting a cat, some people go for a certain look—the cute pug nose and plumy tail of a longhair (Persian, Angora, or whatever); the lithe lines and tawny coloring of the Abyssinian. Or they may be drawn to glossy black cats with chartreuse eyes, or tabbies with their interesting necklace-and-bracelet stripes. But in addition to preference, a little information about the traits of different breeds and types will go a long way toward avoiding disappointment in the cat you choose.

For example, most Siamese do talk a lot in their odd, querulous voices; blue-eyed white cats are often deaf; Abyssinians tend to be active climbers. But even more important than these considerations is beforehand knowledge about the individual cat or kitten you are drawn to. Once you feel a certain chemistry between you and the cat, ask the owner about its personality. If you're adopting from a good shelter, the person who takes care of the cats can tell you something about the animal you're attracted to. The idea is to try not to bring home an animal that will have a hard time adjusting to your ways, and vice versa.

Where to get a cat

Some of us can stand on a street corner in any city and within a matter of minutes find a stray cat. We aren't even looking for one—the cat simply materializes, and once we have locked eyes with it, we find it impossible just to walk away. Sometimes the animal is too wild and frightened to approach. Other times it is twining around our ankles, looking into our face and mewing desperately.

Some friends of mine found a cat in a freezing rain, so help me, on the windowsill of their apartment, eight stories above the ground, with no tree, fire escape, or other access in sight. It could only have been placed there by some thoughtful human being, probably in an adjacent apartment. My friends took the poor kitty in, of course, and in fact still have her, some years later. But it is not unusual to have a cat foisted on you in such a fashion by somebody else. One of my daughter's friends swears that if he ever wanted to get rid of a cat, he'd drop it off on my block.

People who deal professionally with cats caution about bringing home a waif from the street—it is usually diseased and may also be difficult to socialize. And yet, I bet that is precisely the way many cat owners acquired their pets, in spite of all I have just said about choosing a cat.

I believe that compassion is a noble human quality that should be honored, encouraged, and acted upon, and God knows these animals need it. So *do* take home the stray. Just be careful, if you have a cat or cats at home already, not to put it together with them until you've had it checked out by a veterinarian. If it isn't well, you might have to isolate it for a few days. Most cats that have been homeless for very long (weeks or months) have worms, ear mites, fleas, and/or respiratory infections at the very least.

The recently lost or abandoned animal is something else. It may be in very good health indeed, and even if it is terrified or depressed when you find it, it will usually settle in fast and make a wonderful pet. Olivia must have been very recently lost or abandoned when I found her—she was in good condition and had quite obviously been well treated. I tried very hard to find her owner, thinking such a beautiful and gentle cat would surely be greatly missed and sought for, but no one claimed her. (Of course, now I'm glad I wasn't able to locate the owner, but for a long time the thought of a possibly heartbroken person troubled me.)

Pound and humane society cats are often in fairly good shape simply because only healthy, adoptable ones are allowed to live. The classified sections of newspapers are usually full of ads for cats and kittens for adoption. Cats from private homes are fairly likely to be reasonably healthy, maybe even in great shape.

Pet shops are often breeding places for diseases. Some pedigreed cat registries flatly oppose buying from pet shops, urging instead that if you must have a special breed, you buy it directly from a breeder. A good pet shop, however, and there are some, has healthy animals and will give you a guarantee that you can return an animal within a reasonable time if it turns out to be sick or to have a serious personality problem. This is not a happy situation—by that time you may have grown fond of the animal, and also it's hard on a pet to be chosen, taken home to a strange place, and then rejected. But a good shelter will also take returns, and in the long run, it's better to do that than to keep an animal in a home where it's not loved.

The trouble with most pet shops, particularly the large chains, is that they buy their animals wholesale from puppy mills and kitten mills. These mills are disreputable concentration camps for animals where caged dogs and cats produce offspring like machines, and the puppies and kittens are sold like vegetables. The death rate in these places is high, the disease and injury rate is even higher, the shipping conditions horrifying, and the survivors wind up in pet stores that are often no better than the appalling mills they have come from. So, in most instances, if you buy a cat from a pet store, you simply insure the economic success of kitten mills.

Breeders are a mixed lot. Some are enthusiastic and well-informed hobbyists who use considerable professionalism in trying to perpetuate or create certain types of pedigreed cats. They tend to care a lot about their individual animals as well as the excellence of their line. Good breeders often insist that buyers of their cats neuter them, to prevent careless breeding. Among such small entrepreneurs, breeding is careful and limited and probably does not significantly add to the present cat overpopulation situation.

Then, there are breeders who are simply amateurs trying to make a buck. They tend to be interested in cats as a commodity, and some would just as soon sell you a sick animal, or a phony one, whatever they can get away with.

It seems to me the public is in the paradoxical position of having to subsidize, indirectly, with our tax dollars, the cat businesses—the kitten mills, the good and bad pet shops, even to a small extent the good and bad breeders. Some twenty million cats and dogs a year are brought to pounds, shelters, and SPCA's that are supported by municipal funds and public donations. It costs money, our money, to round up homeless cats and bring them to the pounds; it costs money to accept cats turned in to pounds and shelters by owners who no longer want them. It costs money to care for cats until they are adopted, or to euthanize them. Since pounds and shelters are continually overcrowded, 85 percent of these cats have to be killed, at our expense, because homes cannot be found for them. It even costs money to dispose of their bodies.

So on the one hand, while we are paying pounds and shelters to usher some fifteen million cats a year to their deaths because no one wants them, kitten mills and breeders are bringing more and more cats into the world to sell. Does this make sense?

Most of all, however, we are forced to subsidize the ordinary cat owners who allow their pets to breed, or who dump their unneutered pets. We are currently in the midst of a pet overpopulation crisis, thanks largely to people who reply to suggestions of neutering with, "Oh, I would never do that to my cat," or who abandon cats that go forth and increase the stray cat population as long as they live.

Regardless of who is most responsible for the present problem, the fact is that millions of cats are suffering. Millions are euthanized at pounds, humanely or not; other millions wait in cages; and eight or nine times as many more millions are starving on the streets. If people didn't buy cats but adopted them instead, fewer would be bred commercially because the demand would drop. Maybe kitten mills would be phased out. (By the way, you can often find special breeds of cats such as Siamese or Persians up for adoption at shelters.) And most important, if you bail a cat out of a shelter or pound, you save its life.

I suggest that for the present, the most humane and responsible way to acquire a cat is to adopt one.

chapter three

Kitten, Adolescent, and Adult:
How to Mix and Match

The ideal way to have a pair of cats or more that can keep
each other company is, of course, to start out that way—
adopt siblings, or two or three cats that have lived together
and are already friends. But let's say you find yourself with a
single, full-grown indoor cat. Perhaps you have recently
adopted it, or had it for years and its companion has died, or
maybe your household has changed so that now there is
nobody home during the day. For whatever reason, your pet
is alone and you decide to get it a friend or two.

A new kitten rather than an adolescent or adult usually,
though not always, works out best and causes the least
trauma to a resident indoor cat or cats. While an older cat
might hate the kitten, only a real psychotic would actually
harm one. What usually happens is that the kitten will approach the older cat and be rebuffed by a hiss, a growl,
maybe a swat. The kitten will then retreat, only to try again
later. If the older cat is really hostile, the kitten will learn
to keep a respectful distance, and in that case the kindest

thing you can do is bring in another kitten to be its friend. Three cats are a nice number.

Once I brought home a charming kitten I had acquired on the street. A child close to tears had it in a box; he had been sent out to get rid of a litter of kittens and had not been able to find a taker for this one, the last, and was afraid of what might happen to it if he returned home with it. Well, what else could I do? At that time, my children were young and we had only an older indoor cat named Katie, a calm, patient, self-possessed spayed female. I wondered on the way home how she would feel about this newcomer.

"Mommy!" the kitten seemed to cry when it spotted Katie, and ran up to her. Katie made no move to run or to drive the kitten away from her. She simply smelled it over carefully and then casually walked away. Later, she allowed the kitten to nestle up to her, and most amazing, to nurse at her belly. Though she had never had kittens, she mothered the foundling. She looked at us as if to say, "Well, he's a bit peculiar, but I guess it's okay." She also washed him and obviously grew quite fond of him.

Introductions

What intimidates most people and discourages them from adopting a second or third cat is the strange howls and growls cats usually give out with when they first meet. They sound as if they were going to tear each other limb from limb. This warfare seems more intense and is harder to take when you and the cats are all indoors. And it may indeed take longer for indoor cats to get used to a newcomer because they can't really get very far away from each other.

Presumably, a cat feels threatened by what it considers an invasion of its territory by a newcomer, and it may be jealous that the new cat will appropriate the owner's affections. I suppose its feelings are not unlike what a small child seems to feel upon the arrival of a new brother or sister. While some cats, like Katie, are unperturbed, most are considerably upset for the first few days or weeks a new animal is in the home. The new cat, also, is likely to be extremely defensive, being plunked down in another's territory. Some new cats swagger in and take over; most are ill at ease.

Bear in mind that an outdoor cat has usually had encounters with other cats. But to an indoor cat, a new cat may be the first "other" it has laid eyes on since it left its littermates, which it has long forgotten. Naturally, the shock will be greater, and the fright and hostility may be intensified.

When I had indoor-outdoor cats, it never occurred to me to worry seriously about whether my cats would accept newcomers. I simply let them know that each new arrival was welcome, and put down one more food bowl at mealtime, and that was that. I assured the residents that the new pet would in no way affect my relationship with them. They always adjusted, perhaps in part because of my nonchalant attitude. But now that they are totally indoor cats, the tensions are greater when a new cat comes in.

Some cat behaviorists advise having someone else bring a new cat or kitten into your house. They believe this reduces jealousy and feelings of rejection on the part of your resident cat or cats. But whoever brings it in, try to give the newcomer its share of affection and attention when the old pets aren't looking. They need lots of reassuring extra love. Don't force the new and the old on each other; let the initial contacts be casual and natural. Don't try to hold the old cat or the new in your arms during their first encounters. No matter how gentle each is normally, in these tense moments either one might scratch you badly.

If there's a great deal of fuss from either the old or new cat, put them in separate rooms for a few hours and then just leave the door open. Watch out of the corner of your eye to be sure nobody actually hurts anyone, but play it very cool yourself. If there is a lot of noise, even a little fur flying, in the early stages, don't be discouraged. Chances are the cats will calm down, settle in, and even grow to love each other.

Kittens

Should you decide to adopt a kitten as a friend for your single indoor cat, you can look forward to a lot of pleasure. You should also be forewarned. If it has been some years since your own cat was a kitten, you may have forgotten about kittens. I say this only because kittens are so adorable, enchanting, amusing, delightful, and attractive that people don't expect the other-than-darling side of kittens.

How can I seem to be suggesting that anyone avoid the rewarding experience, the fun, of having a kitten as a pet? I'm not at all saying *avoid*, I'm simply saying know what you're getting. Nobody should believe that a pet is wonderful at all times and never a problem. And an animal should not be taken on consignment, but in good faith. It shouldn't be subject to rejection because of the impossible expectations of the owner. I once knew a woman who returned an eleven-week-old kitten within twenty-four hours because, to her surprise and horror, it committed the ghastly sin of jumping onto the kitchen table.

Kittens can get into an awful lot of mischief; they need supervision. Be well aware in advance that with a kitten around, you cannot, for example:

wrap a package,
sort the laundry,
repot a plant,
read a newspaper,
sew on a button,
pack a suitcase,
trim a Christmas tree,

make a bed,
paint a room,
write a letter,
work a jigsaw puzzle,
or put on a pair of pantyhose
in peace.

And there's more than nuisance involved—some of these activities pose dangers to the kitten. Tinsel, for example, can poison a cat; sewing needles can stick in its throat; swallowed string can knot in the intestines (see Chapter Six).

Furthermore, kittens are virtually tireless and you could swear they only sleep when nobody's around. All this can be exasperating enough to the experienced cat lover. It can make a neophyte start looking for a foster home.

When Gina was a kitten, she would sit by the toaster, and if you weren't watching, she would swipe the toast the minute it popped up, run away with it, and eat it, scattering crumbs, under a table. I hung up all the house plants and put away valuable trinkets for a while. I put a latch on the cabinet where the cat food was stored, and a heavy weight on the lid of the garbage can. I had to be creative to avoid continual disciplining.

By the way, when I said earlier that we had Katie when my children were young, I mean Katie was a big, full-grown cat and my youngest child was three when we first got her. We were vigilant about supervising the children until they learned how to be gentle with her. *Never bring a kitten into a house with toddlers.* Little children with the best intentions and kindest hearts in the world can maul a kitten to death, literally.

And adolescents

The behavior of kittens is more or less uniform. They all tend to be frisky, playful, curious, and—unless their mother was fearful and suspicious—outgoing and trusting. They have all the traits I've just told you about. Adolescents (three to seven or eight months old) have all the characteristics of kittens, intensified. What you can tolerate as charming impishness in a little kitten is often less than adorable in an adolescent. The adolescent cat is a lot like a teen-age person—alternately lovable and insufferable.

Sometimes a bouncy kitten or adolescent that you bring in can really wreck the life of an older cat by pestering it endlessly. I have known some well-adjusted, well-established, sociable cats who turned into trembling neurotics, spending their hours trying to find hiding places where they would not be disturbed. These poor animals were forced always to sleep with an eye open because they never knew when they would be pounced on, and could not even use their litter boxes without being ambushed.

No cat should have to endure this for long. The best way to avoid it is to adopt two kittens, or two adolescents, or one of each. You might think that two would simply gang up on the older cat and double the annoyance quotient, but they are far more likely to play-fight with each other than bother the older cat. After all, they are used to playing with their siblings, and they know that they will get a cooperative response from one another. Why waste time, they figure, on the old fuddyduddy?

A formerly two-cat friend of mine yielded to the pitiful plight of an adolescent that had had a hard life on the street. There was surprisingly no personality damage in the new little cat—she was trusting, affectionate, and above all, grateful. At first, she seemed to think that in Paradise, where she surely believed she had landed, her place was considerably below that of the older two. She was very respectful. Albert the Siamese allowed himself to be won over almost at once. Margot, on the other hand, would have none of little Mistletoe and made no bones about hating her.

Poor Margot—some of her loathing for Mistletoe was understandable. As Mistletoe began to feel at home, she became a prankster. One trick the adolescent cat quickly learned was to charge Margot when she was lying peacefully in one of her favorite places—her owner's bed. Mistletoe would zoom around the apartment as if she were on her little motorcycle. Suddenly she would roar into the bedroom and actually glance off the bed where Margot was reclining, exactly as if she were on a BMW going around a racetrack. Margot would spring to her feet, wild-eyed, in a state of shock.

Before long, however, my friend began to notice Margot actually inviting action. For instance, if Mistletoe were lying on a table or chair, Margot would deliberately go and lie on the floor directly beneath her. She would pretend not to notice that Mistletoe was there, but would let her tail twitch tantalizingly. Of course, Mistletoe would be unable to resist. She'd pounce, and the two of them would be off on a tear around the house. My friend found that both Albert and Margot got more exercise after Mistletoe moved in.

So a pesky adolescent is not always a bad thing, even if it shakes up an older cat. Just be observant enough to be sure neither cat is being harmed or made miserable, and remember that the situation is fluid—both kittens and adolescents grow up.

Adult cats

An adult cat is a decided, individual personality and reflects the life it has had, whether it has been well treated and loved or abused and neglected. If you're adopting a grown cat as a companion to your older cat, you might think it makes sense to know something about the personality of the new cat so you can anticipate how the two will react to each other. Forget it. It's impossible to second-guess adult cats.

"Do indoor cats suffer? Are you kidding?"

Wild species of cats often lie this way on the limbs of trees. Perhaps it allows for a fast alert and quick getaway if necessary.

The joys of paper-bagging it. Here, a ferocious lion in its den.

H. Warner Hedgecoth

When it comes to knowing how to relax, cats are the original yoga experts.

Happiness is having a friend to curl up with.

Many adult male cats have fatherly instincts. "Hold still, you little pipsqueak, while I wash your ear," this fellow might be saying.

This handsome, contented, and benign house cat was once a starving, abandoned waif.

John Gajda, Detroit, MI

Sometimes it's best to plan ahead for getting out of a situation before you get yourself into it.

"Now, if I just give this nice shiny thing a little tap . . ."

H. Warner Hedgecoth

You might say this cat is thankful its owners never heard of Atkins, Pritikin, or Scarsdale.

They make enemies or friends of each other for their own reasons, not for ours.

One friend of mine had a cranky cat named Cleopatra. This animal was a beauty, but although she liked her owner very much and would sit in her lap, strangers could not touch her, and neither the owner nor anyone else could pick her up.

My friend tried to get a companion for Cleo. She agreed to take a lovely, innocent, adult female named Velvet who was quite timid, not at all assertive or aggressive. You would think she would be an ideal friend for Cleo—nonthreatening, not bothersome, just a nice quiet companion. But Cleo had murder in her heart from the very first. At one point, Velvet had to flee up the chimney of the fireplace to save herself. At the end of a harrowing week, my friend returned Velvet to her original owner, for Velvet's own safety and sanity.

But a few years later, this friend acquired a swaggering, meddlesome, self-confident kitten—a real holy terror that you would have thought Cleo would hate. She did at first and put up an awful fuss. But after a month or two, she grudgingly accepted him.

Pushkin's owner eventually brought home a friend for him, a sweet-tempered and passive little female cat named Rosebud. One would have thought Pushkin would have quickly come to enjoy the presence of such a nonthreatening Other. Not so. Pushkin launched a campaign of bullying and practical jokes against Rosebud. Finally my friend retrieved Rosebud from under the bed one last time and, much to the poor little cat's relief, traded her in for a three-month-old male foundling. This cat, whom she named Llama, was so grateful to have a home and an owner that he took an awful lot from Pushkin, but he had his limits and would defend himself eventually. Also, for the first ten days or so, my friend lavished extra attention and preference on Pushkin, even to the extent of letting him sleep in her bedroom while the newcomer retired in the kitchen. It worked. Pushkin adopted a rather fatherly attitude toward Llama, and today they are friends. And not being lonely has made a big improvement in Pushkin's temperament.

When young Clarence was introduced into the household that included Thompson Jones and Carla, he was largely ignored by Thompson, the gentle, gigantic, gray neutered male, but Carla complained bitterly about being pestered. And as Clarence grew bigger and heavier, he became increasingly a problem to the small-boned, lightweight Carla. When Clarence would get a stranglehold on her and she couldn't get away, she would scream piteously until one person or another in the house came and chased Clarence away from her.

One day this was going on, with Clarence malevolently pinning Carla to the floor in a game of his own invention, and Carla was yowling helplessly, when suddenly Thompson burst into the room shaking his head. Apparently he had had it. With one powerful swipe, he knocked Clarence across the room. Clarence flew like a cat in an animated cartoon, head over heels, thump against the wall, while Carla fled to safety. Cats work out their own power struggles.

My own three indoor cats all react differently whenever a new cat comes to visit, or when I acquire one I must keep temporarily.

Gina views the newcomer with interest, hisses if it comes too close too quickly, but within a few hours is friendly toward it. Fred looks at the new cat with marked disgust and is grumpy toward it for days, but his general attitude seems to be, "Rise above it. This too shall pass!" Olivia, however, acts as if she's going to have a heart attack, runs from the foreigner, won't let me or anyone else console her, and is out of sorts for days. None of them would ever attack another cat, they simply express their varying degrees of disapproval. Their club has always had a fluctuating membership, however, and I don't think they feel really threatened.

Cautions

Sometimes it happens that the problem with introducing a new cat to be a companion to yours lies not in the animosity of your resident cat toward the newcomer, but the other way around. I'm not talking now about the exuberant kitten or adolescent that annoys an older cat out of mischief, but the really hostile animal that seriously attacks. There have been instances where a new cat has terrorized not just one but several cats together in a household.

Cats, like people, can be really crazy. If you have inadvertently brought in a demented cat that means business against your indoor cat or cats, you have to give up with that one. Don't blame yourself or feel that you can help the situation; just place the poor animal, if you can, in a household with no other cats. If all efforts in that direction are fruitless, and they might be, it's best to have the animal euthanized. An unadoptable animal is better off put gently and painlessly to "sleep" with an overdose of anesthetic by a private veterinarian than going to the pound or animal shelter where it will surely be confused and terrified and eventually be killed perhaps not so humanely.

Lastly, you may decide that what you want as a companion for yourself, your family, and your indoor cat is not another cat but a dog. For information on this combination, see Appendix.

chapter four

Diet:

For the Lounge Lizard

or the Gymnast

Because the world of the indoor cat is circumscribed, meals take on a heightened importance. The cat with access to the garden may choose a variety of diversions that offer a range of stimuli. While the indoor cat manages to amuse itself, especially with your help, meals are clearly high points in its day. Variety in the diet makes the meals more interesting and healthful.

Also, unless you are supervigilant about playing actively with your cat or providing the means that encourage it to play, an adult indoor cat, especially an older one, tends to get lazy and plump. People who allow a pet to become obese are doing the animal a disservice. It is extremely unhealthy and no doubt uncomfortable for it to be grossly overweight. Owners of such cats sometimes say they have no idea why Felix is so fat because they don't overfeed him, but unless Felix has learned to open the refrigerator, thereby becoming the first cat in history to accomplish this feat, he is fat because his owners overfeed him or feed him the wrong food.

A man I know has a marvelous yellow cat named Whiskers that he had overfed till the animal was so blimp-shaped it could barely walk. Then the man took up jogging and became very conscious of his own contours and very proud of the new leanness he achieved. One day his eye fell upon his cat with fresh insight. He put Whiskers on a strict diet. It certainly improved the cat's health and appearance, but all poor Whiskers knew was that he was starving. (What a headache he must have had!) It would have been far kinder and more sensible never to have allowed the animal to reach such a girth in the first place.

I have never known a truly fat kitten or adolescent, indoors or out, and my experience is that you don't have to worry about overfeeding them. They are growing rapidly and are so active, especially if there are two or more, they burn up calories fast. But an adult indoor cat needs both exercise and a proper diet to keep the svelte figure that is its birthright.

How much food how often

An average-size adult indoor cat should eat twice a day, about two ounces (one-third of a regular six-ounce can of cat food or one-fourth cup dry food) at each feeding. If your cat has an unusually big frame or is very active, it might need more than four ounces total a day, in which case try five or six.

In judging how much to feed your cat, be guided by your eye—never mind how many pounds it weighs. Some small-boned cats can be overweight at ten pounds; others—the real hefty bruisers—can carry fifteen pounds and look trim. But if your animal looks fat and feels fat to you, it's fat.

Kittens should be fed at least five small meals daily. In

fact, never let a young kitten go longer than six or seven hours without food during the day; it can go into hypoglycemic shock and die. A newly weaned kitten can pack away a total of eight ounces a day. If your kitten screams for food every time you go into the kitchen, and doesn't vomit or seem bloated, feed it. Taper down as it approaches adulthood, however, so this between-meals snacking doesn't become a habit.

An adolescent cat (three to seven or eight months old) will do best on three meals daily. It can eat as much as twelve ounces daily without batting a whisker. But again, taper down the quantity and number of feedings as it grows up.

Many cats that have been starvelings, like our yellow cat Baxter, never completely lose their anxiety about food, even after they have been given two square meals a day without fail for years and years. Some of these cats never put on excess weight, no matter how much they eat. My advice is to give them little snacks for reassurance when they ask. If you have a number of pets, its hard to feed one without bringing in the whole mob, who don't need the extra tidbits. We used to slip Baxter little treats very quietly and quickly before the others had a chance to realize what was up.

A midnight snack now and then won't hurt your cats, unless they are very overweight. People who want to sleep late the next morning often find this will keep their cats from waking them at their usual breakfast time. I sometimes toss a small handful of dry food into each of my pets' feeding bowls when I go to bed on a weekend night, and they don't get up the next day until I do.

Even though they don't wake me, I believe they are aware that their normal breakfast time has passed. Cats seem to be able to tell time to an amazing degree (and not just mealtimes, either—they seem to know when significant members of the household are due home from work and to notice other regular rhythms of the day). That's why it's a good idea, if possible, to feed your cats at more or less the same hours every day. Why stress them needlessly by making them worry about when something as important (to them) as food is going to appear?

I don't believe in leaving unfinished food for a cat to come back to, even dry food. At my house, the cats either clean their bowls at each feeding, or I pick up what's left, put it back in the can or container, cover it, and put it in the refrigerator for the next meal. Food that's left out attracts bugs. It gets crusty and unappetizing, and no sensible cat will eat it, given a choice. Also, in warm weather, unrefrigerated food may spoil rapidly and make the cat sick.

Incidentally, always cover unfinished cans of food when you put them in the refrigerator; otherwise the food dries up and becomes inedible even though it hasn't spoiled. Also, if it is a pungent type, it might smell up your refrigerator. You don't want your butter tasting of Gourmet Kitty.

Water

Some people don't realize that cats need water. They do, especially in hot weather or in heated houses. Be sure that fresh water in a clean bowl is available to your cat at all times. Take care to wash out the bowl often, as well as refill it, to remove any film or deposit. While dogs generally aren't too fussy about the water they drink, cats are—some cats would let themselves become ill from dehydration before they'd drink dirty water.

When I hear of cats drinking out of the toilet, as some do, I tend to wonder what their drinking bowls look like. Cats that do this may just be quirky, but others may do so when they find the water in the toilet is fresher than that stagnant stuff in their slimy drinking bowl. By the way, don't let a small kitten try to drink or play with the water in the toilet—it could fall in and drown.

Most cats love to watch water drip from a faucet; some even like to get a drink that way. I think it's the action and novelty that intrigues them. A drippy faucet, however, should not be relied on to provide the water your pet needs, and a clean bowl of clean water should always be where your cat can find it.

By the way, while cats normally lap a little water a couple of times a day, excessive drinking can mean that a cat is ill. (See *Symptoms of illness,* in Chapter Seven.)

What to feed

The basic diet of an indoor cat can consist of canned and dry foods in as much variety as the animal enjoys and digests well. The better brands of canned food are at least 10 percent protein and also include some fat, which cats need. Dry foods (little pellets, chow, or flakes that come in boxes) are about 30 percent protein and are also good for the teeth. Canned and dry are both nutritious, and most cats like most brands and flavors. But take it easy in feeding canned fish—too much can make cats deficient in vitamin E, causing a disease called steatitis. Even cats that eat canned fish with vitamin E added have been known to get steatitis, raising the question of whether enough vitamin E was added to the formula, or whether it deteriorates in the can.

There was once a belief that because they are high in ash (mineral) content, dry foods could cause cystitis or urinary blockage, especially in older, neutered males. But new evidence seems to point to obesity and inactivity as the main reasons that some cats are prone to urinary disorders. The basic diet of my cats, including sixteen-year-old Fred, is about one-third dry food.

Makers of dry cat food used to include ash content in the

guaranteed analysis printed on the box or package, along with the amount of protein, fat, crude fiber, et cetera. For some reason, they no longer do. Dry cat foods are relatively high in ash (phosphorus, calcium, and iron particularly—minerals that cats need). Cat food that's low in ash might also have insufficient minerals for adequate nutrition. Whether or not ash is harmful to cats that tend to have urinary problems is not known.

The exact mineral needs of cats have not been definitely established, but it is safe to say that they need small amounts of a wide variety of minerals regularly. That's why a widely varied nutritious diet is best for your cat, and a narrow or single-food diet is harmful.

If you feed your cats mostly dry food, it will appreciate your supplementing it with some fat. Butter, bacon fat, wheat germ oil are good fat sources. One scant teaspoon daily should be enough.

Kittens under twelve weeks old should not be given regular dry cat food because their little teeth aren't strong enough to crunch it. However, they can be fed the dry food that's especially formulated for kittens. Moisten it a little for a very young kitten.

By the way, the cardboard boxes or heavy paper bags the dry foods are packaged in are very vulnerable. A clever cat can smell the contents a mile away and will climb the highest shelf or figure out a way to open the most securely closed cupboard to get at them. I suggest either keeping them in the refrigerator or storing them in large empty coffee cans with tight plastic lids.

In addition to the basic diet, other foods should be given to a cat for nutrition and variety: cottage cheese; yogurt; cooked egg; junior baby meat; cooked meat and fish (cut up); cooked vegetables (no kidding—cats need and like vegetables); wheat germ; cooked chicken hearts, livers, and gizzards (chopped); other cooked organ meats (chopped).

Table scraps (*no bones*) add interesting variety, but a steady diet of table scraps does not provide a cat with the nutrition it needs.

Brewers' yeast (powdered or tablet) is an excellent protein, vitamin, and mineral booster. About one-half teaspoon of powdered, debittered yeast mixed in the cat's food daily, or at least several times a week, is usually enough for a healthy cat. If your cat likes the tablets, feed it all it wants. The tablet form is less potent than the powdered, so it couldn't eat enough to do any harm. Large quantities of tablets are a somewhat expensive way of ensuring your pet's nutrition, that's all.

Cats need fresh vegetables regularly. A cat that goes outdoors satisfies this urge by nibbling grass, weeds, and other plants. An indoor cat may attempt to fill this need by chewing house plants or cut flowers (some suggestions for preventing this are discussed in Chapter Eight). So it's a good idea to mix cooked, cut-up green and yellow vegetables into your cat's food frequently, at least every couple of days. Green beans, peas, celery, lettuce, parsley, spinach, broccoli, carrots, squash, corn are good. (Don't let your cat eat corncobs, though—they're indigestible and could cause blockage.) You might also offer your cat raw vegetables—if it will eat them, they're good for it.

Moist or semidry cat foods (those that come in foil packages) are nutritious enough but high in preservatives, salt, and sugar and generally should be avoided. They are certainly convenient, but the additives are not only nonnutritious but could be harmful if fed as a steady diet.

Some nutrition-conscious people give their cats vitamin tablets to supplement their food. If your cat is healthy and getting a varied diet of nutritious food, vitamin tablets are probably unnecessary (unless your cat is a vegetarian—see below). Healthy cats particularly don't need vitamin C, and they should never be given the ascorbic-acid form of it, for that can irritate their stomachs and cause diarrhea.

Food no-no's:

No bones (can choke a cat to death)

No raw fish (destroys vitamin B₁)

No raw meat (may contain toxoplasmosis, a protozoan parasite)

No raw egg whites (destroys biotin, a B vitamin; yolk is okay, though)

No dog food (deficient in some nutrients cats need)

No very spicy foods (upsets cats' stomachs)

By the way, it's best not to feed a cat, especially a kitten, food directly from the refrigerator—let it come to room temperature. You can hasten this by putting it in an unlit oven (one that has a pilot light) for a while. If it's canned food, you can put the can directly on a very low burner for several seconds to take the chill off. The reason for warming the food is that some cats throw up too-cold food; it must not agree with them. Or, a cat might refuse it because if the food is really cold, the cat can't smell it.

Milk: It is widely believed that cats like milk and that it is good for them. But many cats hate it and would sooner starve than drink it. And in fact, milk gives most cats diarrhea. Small helpings of cream or evaporated milk (say, a couple of tablespoonfuls), however, are good for cats that like it, if they can tolerate it without getting diarrhea.

I have had cats that were true milk freaks. You could not leave a carton of milk unattended for a minute around Baxter. He knew that if he tipped over the carton, all the lovely milk would come spilling out. He would be in such ecstasy lapping it up that he would risk our shouts of rage as we descended on him until we were inches away—then he'd be off with the speed of light.

My cinnamon tabby, Olivia, gets a tablespoon or two of light cream or half-and-half after her breakfast, and I think it is one reason her coat is so glossy. She comes back into the kitchen after all the cats have gone about their business and sits in front of the refrigerator awaiting her treat. (Fred and Gina check in occasionally to see what she's getting, and then walk away—they don't like cream.) Olivia also comes running every time she hears me pour a cup of tea or coffee, for she knows that milk will follow, and she apparently figures there's no harm in asking. Sometimes it's hard to refuse her, but I'm afraid more would not agree with her.

Gourmets

A word about exotic tastes: Cats are such individualistic animals; it is quite common for them to develop passions for unusual foods—unusual, that is, and even bizarre for cats to like. I've heard of a cat named Menelaus that loves the brine from jars of stuffed olives; his owner gives him a tablespoon or two now and then, and he seems none the worse for it. He also goes wild for black raspberry ice cream. And I once had a cat that adored bananas.

Indoor cats are more likely than others to have exotic tastes because they generally live close to their human beings, and when we have snacks, they are right there begging for a taste. I don't think it does any harm to let them sample a bit, within reason. But it could create a problem if you let a cat get hooked on, say, caviar. And don't let your cat's gourmet tastes and snacks interfere with its regular meals.

The vegetarian cat

While I myself am a vegetarian, I have had no firsthand experience with vegetarian diets for cats, nor have I found much in the literature about the subject. But my research has led me to believe that a cat could be healthy on a meat-free diet so long as it got some animal protein and ample vegetable protein every day. From 35 to 50 percent of a cat's diet should be protein. But if you think a vegetarian diet is off the wall, take a look at the ingredients listed on a can or box of regular cat food—you'll see that a cat who eats cat food as its main diet gets a lot of vegetable protein anyway.

Good animal protein sources (other than meat) are eggs, cottage cheese, yogurt, and cream or milk (but give milk sparingly; see above). High vegetable protein sources are soy beans, sprouts (all kinds—wheat, alfalfa, mung bean, lentil, et cetera), yeast, and bean curd (tofu).

Cats particularly need vitamins A, B, and E. Cod liver oil (a scant teaspoon daily) or one 10,000 IU vitamin A capsule every other day will supply the necessary A. Egg yolks, cooked carrots, and corn also contain this vitamin. Brewers' yeast (¼ to ½ teaspoon daily) supplies the B vitamins as well as some protein. Whole grains—oatmeal, corn meal, brown rice, barley, farina—are good B sources. Wheat germ (one teaspoon daily) or wheat germ oil (½ teaspoon daily) is a good source of vitamin E, as is peanut oil. Or you might give your pet a 50 IU vitamin E capsule daily or a 100 IU capsule every other day.

Don't forget your pet's vegetable needs also—cooked corn, peas, green beans, spinach, and other green vegetables. And unless the yeast you buy contains zinc and kelp, you will want to supply that. You can break up a 10 mg zinc tablet and give the cat 1 or 2 mg daily; as for kelp, get the powder and give your cat ½ teaspoon daily.

It's entirely possible a cat might thrive on such a diet. But when you first try it, phase it in gradually and watch your animal carefully for signs of diet deficiency—weakness, dull coat, diarrhea, lethargy, nervousness, weight loss, running eyes, or ulcerated mouth. One reason I think nutritional deficiency is unlikely, however, is that the domestic cat is probably descended not from the jungle or savannah dwellers but from the Egyptian cat, which was a little desert animal the Egyptians domesticated. Its original wild ancestors surely didn't get a diet high in meat.

Naturally, if your cat has been living on a diet that includes a lot of fresh meat, or canned cat foods with meat, it may not immediately gobble up a meal of cottage cheese, alfalfa sprouts, and spinach sprinkled with wheat germ. You'll have to add the new ingredients gradually, increasing the amounts slowly. This gives you time to observe your pet's health, as its body adjusts to the change in diet. If you have a kitten, now is a good time to get it used to vegetables and nonmeat protein.

There's evidence that suggests a largely vegetarian diet is especially good for an old cat (see Appendix).

Feeding bowls

Every cat should have its own bowl. When two or more cats have to share a bowl, the fastest and most aggressive eaters get most of the food, and the other cats may go hungry. Cats differ greatly from one another in their eating styles— some wolf down the food, others eat fastidiously and like to linger a bit over a meal. Watch your cats while they eat to be sure every cat gets to finish as much as it wants, without interference.

Feed your cats in a relatively quiet spot away from kitchen noise and traffic. Each cat should be allowed to eat undisturbed—don't pet it or allow the dog to bother it, and don't let a kitten or other speedy eater rush over and stick its head into the bowl of a cat that is still trying to eat.

Space the feeding bowls a foot or two apart. A cat will often try to check out another's bowl, to be sure the other hasn't got something good that it hasn't got. Discourage this by gently moving the investigating cat back to its own bowl. Except for raising its head once in a while to chew or meditate, a feeding cat should tend to business till it has finished. When it walks away, put any uneaten food back in the refrigerator and wash the bowl (see *How much food how often,* above).

I once knew a man who insisted that his cats had to be fed right next to their litter box, which he was negligent about changing. Many times the poor animals walked away in disgust, unable to enjoy their food. A repugnant odor can cause a cat to starve itself into severe malnutrition.

Although our cat Katie befriended the kitten I brought in, and even mothered it, she was not above playing a practical joke on it. The first time we fed the kitten, we gave it a bowl next to hers. Katie began to eat her dinner, then looked up and saw the kitten gobbling away next to her. Deliberately, Katie lifted her paw and whacked the kitten on the top of its head. Of course the kitten's face went down into the food, and it got stuff all over its nose and in its eyes and whiskers. After a brief sputter, it went right on eating, but we moved its bowl farther away.

One of our houseguest cats tended to growl softly all the while he ate. Although the cats' bowls were spaced well apart, and nobody was paying any attention to him, I think because he wasn't used to eating with the others, he imagined that someone might try to steal his food. Hence the little warning growl, just in case.

Our calico cat Becky removed each bite of food daintily from her bowl and ate it off the floor. I guess it tasted better to her that way. I saw no reason, or any way, to prevent her from doing this. I just put her bowl on a newspaper, which I changed often, or gave the floor around her bowl a swipe with a wet paper towel after she had finished.

Ceramic or glass bowls are better than plastic, by the way. Some cats are allergic to plastic. One symptom of this allergy is paleness and loss of pigmentation of the nose.

Be sure to wash your cats' bowls after each meal, for simple hygiene and also to protect the pets from the bacteria that form on an unclean bowl. But don't use a strong detergent or cleanser. Cats hate the smell, and if it's not rinsed off totally it could make them sick.

Feeding problems

Every now and then you'll hear of a pet that will eat nothing, its owners insist, but some single, usually luxurious food. This means a spoiled cat, and an unhealthy one. One lady I know tells me that her little Princess won't touch anything but chicken livers in cream sauce. What she really means is that she rather enjoys cooking for her cat, I guess. There's no harm in the cooking, but a one-dish-only cat does not get all the vitamins and minerals it needs, and too much of others.

Variety not only makes meals more interesting to a cat but helps assure it's getting the proper nutrients.

Sometimes when you try to add variety to your cat's diet, you're rebuffed. You put down a new food in its bowl, and the animal sniffs carefully, then with studied and majestic disdain, goes through the motions of covering it up. Since we all know what a cat normally covers up, this gesture is an eloquent expression of what the cat thinks of the food. It doesn't necessarily mean there's anything wrong with the food. If a can of cat food is spoiled, you'll know it—the top of the unopened can is rounded, pops when you open it, and the food is foamy and smells putrid.

But if your cat doesn't want the new food, there's no point in forcing the issue. Either throw out the food, give it to a cat that likes it, or (this is sneaky but often works) mix tiny amounts of it in with something the cat does like. The cat may eat it unknowingly, or eat it grudgingly because it is mixed with the other. However, your pet may do as my Olivia does when I give the cats a treat of cooked chicken livers. I know she doesn't like them, but they're very nutritious, so I mix hers in with other food. When she's finished, I'll find her bowl empty except for a little pile of well-licked but intact chicken liver bits.

When an adult cat passes up a meal occasionally, it is not necessarily a cause for alarm. The cat may simply not be hungry for reasons unrelated to illness. If an adult cat in its usual surroundings stops eating for a day or two, try to tempt it with its favorite foods. But if it still won't eat for three or *at the most* four days, it is most likely sick and you should take it to a veterinarian.

If a kitten stops eating for less than a day—if it refuses more than *two or three meals*—this means big trouble. You must take it to a vet without delay.

Refusal to eat is a symptom of so many different illnesses, there is no way you can diagnose and treat it without professional help.

A sick cat that refuses food should be coaxed, hand-fed, or spoon-fed. No matter how much time this takes, you must do it. The animal needs food as well as whatever medicine the veterinarian has prescribed. The gourmet cat Menelaus was pulled through an illness by owners who sat on the floor and spoon-fed him every bite. If they didn't, he simply wouldn't eat. When a cat feels really rotten, eating may be just too much trouble. This attention from a caring owner can mean the difference between a sick cat that makes it and one that doesn't.

If the cat eats from your hand but then vomits everything up, by the way, it needs medicine to control the vomiting. Tell your vet immediately.

Vomiting, by itself, can mean nothing—or everything. If a cat throws up after a meal occasionally, it is not necessarily sick. The vomiting might be caused by hair balls and have nothing to do with the food it ate. But vomiting that persists

—several times in one day, or once every day for several days—is a danger signal, and your cat needs medical attention.

My Gina eats virtually anything and everything with such zest and has such dependably good digestion that if she throws up a meal, I can expect trouble and I watch her carefully for further symptoms. One day she vomited forcefully, right after eating, although she seemed well in every other way. When she did it a second time, again after eating, I didn't waste time but took her to the veterinarian. The vet discovered she had tonsillitis, caused by impacted anal glands. When Gina washed herself, her mouth and throat became irritated, the tonsils got infected, and swallowing food made her regurgitate. So a cat's vomiting may not even have anything to do with the food you're giving it or even with its digestive system, but indicate that something else entirely is wrong (see Chapter Seven). Know your cat.

Vomiting may also simply mean your cat is emotionally upset. Fred sometimes vomits when he sees me packing a suitcase. Olivia will vomit when a strange cat is in the house. In cases like that, soothe your pet and don't worry unless the vomiting persists.

chapter five

Routine Upkeep:
Hygiene and Grooming

When it comes to cleanliness and keeping up appearances, the domestic cat is in a class by itself among all mammals (including us people, seems to me). Your indoor cat, however, will need your cooperation if it is to exercise its instinctive self-care and also if you are to enjoy your pet's fastidious ways to the fullest.

Daily or regular care will involve you mainly in three ways: litter-boxkeeping, brushing, and nail clipping, for your pet will of course use its box, shed, and sharpen its claws. The outdoor cat buries its wastes, loses much of its excess hair in the bushes or grass, and sharpens its claws on the back fence. You have to make a few substitute arrangements for your indoor cat.

The litter box

The first thing to decide before you get a litter box for your cat is where you are going to keep it. You don't want to buy one and then discover it won't fit in the only place you want to put it. For starters, do not plan to keep the box where the cat eats or sleeps. Your pet will refuse either to eat or to use the box—and it certainly will reject the bed. Secondly, get the biggest box that can be accommodated in the space you choose for it.

Obviously, some out-of-the-way spot the cat can get to easily is best—a back hall, mud room, or accessible porch is ideal. The basement is fine if you can provide a way for your cat to get down there when someone has closed the door. Apartment dwellers usually have to place their cat's box in a bathroom, closet, or the kitchen, and keep it extra clean. Bear in mind that cats do like privacy, and if you put the box in a too noisy or busy place, the pet may choose its own quiet spot.

If the only place for your cat's litter box is some plainly visible spot, you might be tempted to try one of those funny little "houses" that look like dollhouses, are sold in some pet supply stores, and are specifically made to conceal litter boxes. But I must warn you that what usually happens with those is that, because the air can't circulate in and over the box, the odors become concentrated and intense, and eventually permeate the house itself. I think, in general, they are more trouble than a regular open box that is kept tidy. However, a covered litter box, or one with very tall sides, is necessary if you have a male cat that urinates standing instead of crouching. Not many but some males do that. It is not anything you can correct, and the animal is not trying to bug you.

A cardboard carton or wood box is not practical as a litter box unless you can replace it every few days, because it will become damp and odoriferous, and then fall apart. A plain plastic or galvanized metal dishpan is okay. The typical commercial box is molded plastic with a hinged lid made with a lip that prevents some of the litter from scattering.

Some cats scratch more enthusiastically than others, and you may even want to set the litter box in a larger carton with sides, to help reduce the flying litter. Just be sure, if you have a kitten, that the box isn't too deep for it to hop into easily.

You can buy plastic litter-box liners, though I have found that cats often rip them in their scratching, and then when you empty the box, the stuff falls through the tears. Thick layers of newspaper work better in my cats' box.

The typical kind of litter is made of clay. Unfortunately, it exudes clouds of fine dust when you pour it, which settles over everything nearby. Less dusty is the kind made in pellets of either alfalfa or other organic material. Some cats aren't particular which kind you put in their box, but others are very fussy, so let your cat's preference be your guide.

Pour two or three inches of litter in the box; don't fill the box to the top or you'll soon find as much litter scattered outside as in the box. Use a slotted spoon or scoop to sift out the solid matter daily, and flush it down the toilet. (Be careful not to flush much of the litter with it—you might stop up the plumbing.) Stir the litter in the box daily to allow it to dry out—that way you can minimize the frequency with which the litter must be changed.

How often you have to change the box depends on how many cats and how many litter boxes you have. For my three indoor cats, I change their box every other day. Also, about every ten days or two weeks I scrub it out with warm water and detergent. I keep the box on the floor of a storage closet, with one solid deodorizer beside it and another stick-on kind on the bottom of the shelf directly over the box. There's no cat box smell in my apartment. The only drawback to my placement of the box is the need to remind my guests, cleaning woman, or cat sitters to always leave the closet door open a cat-sized crack.

Naturally, one cat tends to relieve itself just when company is due to arrive. Before the odor can waft through the apartment, I tackle it with a deodorant spray, open a nearby window, and wave the door open and shut a few times.

I can't stress too much the necessity and desirability of keeping the box clean. This mildly onerous job is probably the biggest single discourager of people contemplating taking on an indoor cat—and perhaps a reason some people dump their pets. For one thing, a dirty box acquires a pungent smell that permeates the house. For another thing, cats being the fastidious creatures they are, they will quickly take to relieving themselves somewhere else around the house if their box is disgusting to them. A dirty box is probably the major reason for a cat to break litter-box training (see Chapter Eight). Some cats will kindly go in the bathtub or other easy-to-clean spot; other cats may choose a pile of shoes at the back of a closet, or the fireplace, or a corner of the carpet.

Your cat's litter box, by the way, is the place where some of the first signs of illness may show up. Diarrhea, constipation, bloody stool, frequent urination, and urinary blockage are all problems you must attend to—in some cases by just a change of diet, but more likely by an immediate trip to the veterinarian (see Chapter Seven). Keep an eye out for such signals as the cat crouching in the box straining to urinate or defecate—that's a sure sign of trouble and calls for quick medical treatment. Just as our human gastrointestinal system is always of primary concern to our physician when we're sick, a cat's is an important barometer of the state of its health.

It's good to be on the lookout automatically whenever you change your cat's litter box; chances are everything will always be fine, but you don't want to let an important symptom go overlooked. Veterinarians often shake their heads over the inattention of cat owners who let an illness go undiscovered or unattended until it is so advanced that the animal can't be saved. This opportunity for early notice of trouble is one reason indoor cats live longer and in better health than outdoor cats. Even when you have several cats who share a litter box, a bloody stool alerts you to watch carefully to discover which cat is suffering.

Litter-box training

Kittens are famous for being easy to train—in fact, if their mother is an indoor cat, she trains them to the litter box herself. When you first bring a kitten into your house, however, show it the box frequently for a few days till it can remember where it is. You might even gently make scratching motions in the litter with its front paws a few times to give it the idea.

If you do adopt a kitten or cat that has not been trained, keep a close eye on it during the first hours it is in your house. When you see it begin to search out corners and sniff around in an agitated way, put it in the box. If it makes a mistake before you can stop it, put the stool (or the paper towel you wipe up the puddle with) in its box and show it to the animal, then leave it there—it helps the cat remember that's the place.

It's important to have several, easily accessible boxes at first, especially for a kitten, so it doesn't have to run all over trying to remember where the "bathroom" is. A kitten, like a child, waits till the last minute anyway and then makes a frantic dash for it. The cat will gradually come to favor one box, and then you can phase out the others if you want to.

I don't know where the notion originated that the way to housebreak a cat is to rub its nose in its mistake. Some people even think you should spank the animal at the same time as you are rubbing its nose in its stool or puddle. This belief is so wrong, so cruel, and so dumb, I can't understand its popularity except that it provides an outlet for the owner's rage. What it really accomplishes is to make the animal a nervous wreck and cause it to hate and fear you. It will not train it.

If your animal is resisting training, there is something you aren't doing that you should—or you are doing something you shouldn't. If the cat is healthy, its refusal to use the box is not obstinacy on its part. You have overlooked something (see Chapter Eight). In fairness, though, I admit I've heard from reliable sources that some long-haired cats may be difficult to train. If you're having trouble with a Persian, it may not be your fault at all—you might just have to be more patient than with other cats.

If a kitten or cat does not catch on quickly, you might have to confine it for a few days in the place where its box is. Bring it out, of course, to be fed, held, and played with, but when you're not giving it your attention, confine it. Also, if freedom is a reward for the cat's using its box, the good habit will be reinforced. It will also help if you make other, attractive places such as clothes closets or the linen closet inaccessible and therefore nontempting by keeping the doors closed. When the cat is out in the open, it's easier to watch for the moment when it should be put in the box. Every time the animal uses its litter box, reward it with praise and petting. Not for nothing did B. F. Skinner have his successes with behavior modification.

For information on how to deal with breaking training, see Chapter Eight.

Your cat's coat

All indoor cats need regular brushing, for several reasons: to keep hair off furniture, rugs, and clothing, and to keep the animal from swallowing an excess of hair when it washes itself. Short-haired cats shed about as much as long-haired, though they don't need so much combing. Indoor cats shed not seasonally but year-round. Frequent brushing will not only keep down the shedding, it will go a long way toward keeping the animal's coat and skin in healthy condition—and beautiful.

Indoor cats are particularly susceptible to dandruff because of living in heated houses and apartments. A cat whose favorite winter spot is on or by a radiator almost surely will suffer from dry skin and dandruff. In addition to regular brushing, one way to combat dandruff is to be sure the animal gets enough fats in its diet. You might add ½ teaspoon of wheat germ oil or debittered Brewers' yeast to its food daily. Petromalt is a good coat conditioner, too; it comes in a tube—you squeeze out ¼ to ½ inch on your finger and put it back of the cat's lower or upper front teeth. (Some cats like the taste; Fred will lick it off my finger.)

Most cats enjoy being brushed—in fact, when I brush Gina or Fred (or my dog Dandelion), Olivia comes running and tries to get herself between the brush and the other animal. Start brushing a cat, by the way, as early in life as possible, even a very young kitten, to get it accustomed to the feel. A rubber brush is recommended—never one with wire bristles, which ruin the hair. Long-haired cats must be combed as well.

A cat's coat, like its digestive and urinary systems, is a barometer of its general health. If, in spite of your frequent brushing, in spite of the addition of a coat-conditioning dietary supplement, your pet has persistent dandruff, is scratching excessively, or is shedding clumps of hair, it probably has dermatitis. This is a general term for inflammation of the skin and can be caused by parasites, an allergy, some kind of infection, stress, perhaps a hormonal imbalance. There are so many causes of dermatitis, you must take your cat to a veterinarian for diagnosis and treatment (see Chapter Seven). Above all, don't bathe it—you might irritate an already existing condition.

Bathing a cat

Under normal conditions, there is no reason for bathing an indoor cat. Even if its coat gets a little dusty now and then, the cat will most likely clean itself up. If necessary, you can give it a once-over with a warm, wet washrag (well wrung out).

One sign of illness in a cat is failure to wash. Stray cats are as likely to be dirty because they are sick as from living in alleyways, basements, abandoned tenements, and vacant lots. These cats usually feel so hopelessly bad from parasites or respiratory infections that they give up trying to keep themselves clean.

Baxter, the starving yellow cat we took in soon after we moved to the garden apartment, was so filthy that one of the first things I did with him was put him in the kitchen sink and give him a bath. He was so weak and undernourished at that time that he couldn't do more than struggle faintly and mew piteously. When he grew strong and lithe as a steel spring, we never could have managed it. But, interestingly enough, we never had to, because he became fanatically fussy about his appearance. He would wash and groom his coat until every shining hair was in place, and then work on his footpads till they were pink and spotless. Then he'd wet his front paw and do a cleaning number on the insides of his ears. My other cats sometimes let their ears get a little dirty from being out in the yard a lot in the polluted air and dusty shrubbery—but not Baxter! Poor fellow, I think he believed that keeping himself scrupulously clean was somehow a requirement for his keeping his good home with us. (See *Ear grooming*, below.)

Generally, the only occasion for bathing an indoor cat would be if it got toxins on its fur—in which case it would lick itself and swallow the poison. Common household substances such as paint, polishes, insecticides, and the like are poisonous (see Chapter Six). Or, if you adopt a stray that's badly infested with fleas, a bath might be necessary.

Put cotton in your cat's ears, a drop of mineral oil in each eye, and use a mild soap or good tearless shampoo. Don't put the animal in the tub or sink with the water running, which will scare it and make it frantic. Put it in warm water just deep enough to get it thoroughly wet, but not so deep as to make it fear you are trying to drown it. If you put a window screen in the tub with the cat, by the way, it will dig its claws into that instead of into you.

Start washing at its head and neck and work back to the tail. Rinse thoroughly to be sure to get all the soap or shampoo out. Then wrap the cat in towels and dry it thoroughly. Keep it in a warm room so it doesn't get chilled.

Your cat's nails

When a cat rakes a wood or upholstered surface with its claws, it is actually stripping away an outgrown sheath that covers each claw, to make room for the sharp new claw that has grown in underneath. This is a perfectly normal, continuing activity, like the manicuring of our own fingernails. Every indoor cat owner finds the little hollow, sloughed-off nail coverings around the house. When the cat performs this raking or scratching, it looks to us as if it is sharpening its claws—and the newly grown nail is certainly sharp.

If your pet insists on using your furniture for this purpose, it becomes a behavior problem. Suggestions on how to deal with this, including a discussion of scratching posts and the question of declawing, are in Chapter Eight.

However, even if your indoor cat leaves your rugs, upholstery, table legs, and cane and wicker furniture alone, you may want to keep its nails trimmed anyway as a matter of routine grooming. There are good reasons for this: When you're wearing only a thin bathrobe and your pet jumps into your lap, its nails can feel like little needles. Or when it's nesting on a woolly blanket at the foot of your bed, it can pull the threads with its sharp claws.

Cats have a well-known habit of kneading with their front paws when they're happy and cozily ensconced on something soft and warm. Alternating their feet, they flex their toes, extending and retracting the claws. This instinct may go back to earliest kittenhood, when the infant cat kneaded its mother's belly as it nursed to stimulate the flow of milk. In fact, my cat Gina gets glassy-eyed with contentment and puts her nose down close to whatever she is kneading, underscoring the memory she must have of being close to her mother as a tiny kitten. A cat that loves its owner often displays this impulse to knead when sitting on its owner's lap. In fact, all my cats are lap sitters, and each is likely at any time to settle down, purring, on me or any seated human being it is attracted to. And when it gets carried away with affection and comfort, it may knead.

For this reason, I routinely clip my cats' nails, and recommend that you do the same, even if your cat is a perfectly trained scratching-post user. You can buy an inexpensive clipper for this purpose at any pet supply store. Or use regular human nail clippers. (Don't use a dog nail clipper—too big. You'll hurt the cat.)

The way to use this device is to press the cat's toes, one at a time, so the claw protrudes. Then snip off only the sharp tip, taking care not to clip so much that you get the pink vessel in the claw. (If you do that, you'll hurt the cat badly.) Always snip with the clippers aimed from above or below the claw, never across it. It's usually only necessary to do the front paws.

The earlier in life you can accustom your cat to having its nails clipped, the better. Most cats dislike this little operation and will struggle. I try to approach mine when they're sleeping off their dinner, and do it so gently and quickly I can get both front paws done before they've waked up enough to protest. A once-a-week clipping takes no time at all once you get the hang of it.

Ear grooming

Routine care of your cat's ears is tricky. The ears are so delicate you can easily harm them, and also it's hard to tell the difference between normal wax and dirt on the one hand and mites or infection on the other. Veterinarians point out that the anatomical construction of cats' ears seems to set the scene for ear problems.

As a good rule of thumb, don't fool with your cat's ears if:

1) the cat is shaking its head or holding it at a funny angle,
2) the cat is pawing at its ear,
3) the ear appears red, hot, or swollen,
4) there is a musty odor from the ear, or
5) the matter in the ear is thick and caked.

Those symptoms should be shown to a veterinarian because they mean trouble.

If the veterinarian finds ear mites, simple little parasites that look like black wax, they are common and can be gotten rid of by faithful and persistent treatment—by you. Other problems may call for drops in the ear, which the vet will prescribe (see Chapter Seven).

Indoor cats, of course, are far less liable to have ear problems than cats that go outdoors. Also, cats seem to vary in their susceptibility to ear problems, just like people. My cat Olivia's ears are pristine and I never touch them; Gina's need a little wiping out once in a great while—say, every six months or so; but Fred's ears have chronic wax and need cleaning about once a month.

If the vet finds only dirt or wax in your cat's ears, you can clean them out regularly yourself, provided none of the above symptoms is present. Use cotton swabs dipped in baby oil or mineral oil, never soap and water. (As I mentioned earlier, should you have to bathe your cat, protect its ears with cotton so you don't get water in them.) Moisten the swab with oil and gently clean the ear's contours, using a clean swab with each application. Don't poke way in the ear—you might damage it.

Care of the teeth

Fortunately, a healthy cat that's fed a good diet isn't likely to need much teeth care. Some veterinarians do recommend wiping your cat's teeth every couple of weeks with a wad of cotton or a child's toothbrush soaked in baking soda or milk of magnesia in order to prevent the formation of tartar. This might be a good idea, because an accumulation of tartar can make the animal's breath smell bad and also eventually, if the tartar builds up, can cause gum problems.

A couple I know had a cat, Salomé, that used to follow one or the other of them into the bathroom at night and brush its own teeth. The owner would hold the cat's own toothbrush for it, and the cat would rub its teeth—first on one side and then the other—against the bristles.

An older cat, say over ten years, might need regular professional teeth cleaning by a veterinarian. The vet will most likely examine the animal's teeth whenever he or she examines the animal for any reason, including its annual checkup. If the teeth need scraping, it may be necessary to anesthetize the animal, depending on its sensitivity and anxiety level and the veterinarian's patience.

I once had a strange experience with a cat who belonged to some people I knew slightly and was visiting for the first time. They had a middle-aged cat who was crouched in a kitchen window, uttering cries at more or less regular intervals.

"What's the matter with your cat?" I asked.

"Oh, nothing," they said. "He just wants to go outside." The cat didn't look to me as if it wanted to go out—it looked miserable, not agitated. "Well, he hasn't eaten much in the last couple of weeks," they admitted.

As I was stroking the animal, it just occurred to me to look in its mouth. Sure enough, there was a huge, swollen, greenish-gray spot on the lower gum, right under the fang on one side. I showed this to the cat's owners, who were appalled. The man's reaction was to suggest that he get a pair of pliers and yank the offending tooth out. Fortunately, his wife didn't agree to that idea. I asked if I could try something to bring down the swelling, and when they said go ahead, I began to soak wads of paper towel in very warm running water and apply them to the cat's gum. The poor beast began to stretch its head toward my hand and open its mouth so I could get at the sore place better. This seemed odd in itself, because from the looks of it, the gum should have been terribly tender, like an abscess.

Then I noticed pieces of fur were beginning to appear on the paper towel. Further investigation revealed that what I had thought was the gray-green of infected tissue was simply matted cat fur stuck under the gum, which the warm water applications were loosening. The whole problem was that there was a space where the gum had receded around the tooth, and it had become impacted with fur when the animal washed itself. The gum apparently hurt when the cat tried to chew, so it had stopped eating. I kept working until I had cleaned out the whole area, removing maybe a thimbleful of solidly impacted fur. The cat's relief was obvious. It then ate a whole can of cat food. My purely accidental discovery was a lucky one; we all felt better.

I've told you this story simply to point out the advantage

of checking your pet's mouth regularly, to be sure its teeth and gums are in good shape.

If you follow a routine of simple, regular grooming care of your cat, you'll be rewarded with a sleek and handsome animal that fits into your house with minimal trouble. Your good attentions will also be reflected in the health of your cat and fewer necessary trips to the veterinarian.

chapter six

Safety:
The High-rise Syndrome
and Other Hazards

Since it won't get lost, trapped, hit by a car, torn up by dogs, hurt by sadistic people, fall into a roaring river, or get zapped with porcupine quills, the indoor cat faces far fewer dangers than one that has access to the outdoors. Nevertheless, you'd be surprised how much trouble an indoor cat can get into. One of the reasons you'd be surprised, I suspect, is that most books on cat care, even otherwise excellent ones, scarcely mention that most common of killers of indoor cats: the open window. The widespread belief that cats don't fall out of windows is perhaps the most pernicious myth that brings death and injury to indoor pets.

The high-rise syndrome

One hot Sunday last summer when I went out to walk Dandelion, the doorman of our building was somewhat excited and eager to tell me something. He pointed to a tear in the canopy over the sidewalk at the front door.

"Guess how that got there," he said. I said I couldn't imagine.

"Cat fell out a window," he announced. "Nine stories, and went right through the canopy!"

"My God," I exclaimed. "Where is the cat? Did it live? Whose cat is it?"

"It lived, didn't even seem hurt—but was sure scared," our doorman replied. "It ran into the lobby. Its owner, 9D, is away, so the super called the ASPCA and they came and got it."

Poor kitty, I thought—that's probably the end of it, because our ASPCA has a record of haphazardly "euthanizing" animals, especially injured ones, before their owners have a chance to claim them. But luck was with this animal for the second time today. Its owner, a Miss Harris, came home that evening and went up and collected her amazingly uninjured and luckily not-yet-euthanized pet.

I saw Miss Harris one day soon after that and inquired how her cat was. Then I launched the subject, as tactfully as possible, of the high-rise syndrome. This likable and intelligent young woman, like millions of other devoted cat owners, had truly believed that cats have a special sense of balance and do not fall from windows, roofs, or terraces.

"It must really be a widespread old wives' tale," she exclaimed. "I remember my parents, also my grandmother, saying that cats never fall. Our cats at home never fell out of trees. I guess windowsills are different."

Exactly. A cat can dig its claws into a tree limb and hang on. It cannot dig its claws into brick or concrete. And while cats seem not to have much fear of heights, this trait may have caused them more accidents than it has saved them from.

Cats have a pelvic structure that causes them to walk nearly a straight line, with each foot stepping almost directly in front of the other, rather than parallel steps. This enables them to walk along the tops of fences or pick their way daintily across the mantel—but it does not give them an infallible sense of balance.

Therefore, a cat sitting in an open, unscreened window is in serious danger. A cat chasing a moth or fly through a room with an open window can sail right out after its prey. A cat smelling the flowers in a windowbox on the ledge of an apartment terrace, or a cat investigating the railing at the edge of a sun roof, is similarly at risk.

In addition to the notion that cats don't fall, there is a collateral belief that they can fall from great heights and survive. This myth is hard to dispute because there are, in fact, true instances of cats surviving incredible falls. One book on cat care, written by a veterinarian, addresses only a short paragraph to the high-rise syndrome, and instead of firmly warning owners to protect their pets, gives dazzling statistics about the recorded heights from which cats have fallen and lived—thereby creating the impression that if your cat does fall, it probably won't get hurt. If you believe this, I recommend that you spend the first few warm days of spring at any urban veterinary hospital and count the broken or dying cats that are brought in.

"Every spring before the air conditioners go on, and again in Indian summer, in come the high-rise cases by the dozen," remarked one experienced city veterinarian.

Indoor stairwells are only a very small danger, because while a cat might make a jump for the railing and miss, it probably would not be seriously hurt in a fall from one floor to the next. Of course, if the stairwell had a drop of several stories, it could be just as perilous to a cat as an open window several stories above the ground.

I hate to admit it, but my beloved Fred was once the victim of an open window in our apartment. The window had been opened from the bottom, without my knowledge, by a youngster who was visiting my son, then a teenager. My son carelessly didn't notice, the kids went out, Fred got curious, and the tragedy happened. Many months and three operations later, after extreme discomfort on Fred's part and distress on our part, after much expense and trouble, Fred was walking almost normally, his leg bone secured in place with pins and wires. He's a masterpiece of modern veterinary orthopedic surgery.

Fred's fall was six stories. Miss Harris' cat fell nine stories to a canopy. But a cat in the building next door fell five stories to its death. So my advice is to be skeptical about the tales of how far cats have fallen and survived. Even if some of the individual claims are true, they only distort the facts— that a cat that falls from an open window, a roof, or terrace is in all probability going to be badly hurt or killed.

One factor that confuses the issue is the cat's famous ability to land on its feet. This much is true: cats are born with an amazing ability to right themselves quickly in midair so that no matter what position they start their falls in, they land feetfirst. (However, a cat that's held on its back and dropped just a few feet will land on its back or side because it hasn't had enough time to turn.) This skill at twisting the body when free-falling—a difficult thing to do—must fascinate scientists because much has been studied and written about it. But many people mistakenly believe that it will protect a falling cat from death or injury. Too bad this isn't true, or so many unprotected cats wouldn't wind up in the animal hospital or in cat heaven.

Screen your windows. If you open them from the top, open them just a few inches, not a foot or two that will attract the cat's interest and encourage it to climb up and perch on the top of the frame. Screen your terrace completely. Keep your cat off the roof or fire escape. These attentions are far less costly and time-consuming than the vet care your cat would require if it fell—and survived.

Now, if your cat should fall: Place it gently in a cat carrier or a box (or on a blanket or coat, if necessary), keep it warm and quiet, and get it to a veterinarian immediately. Even if it doesn't seem to have any broken limbs, it should be checked for internal injuries and treated for shock. Don't let anyone try to give it a sip of water or brandy or any well-meant home remedies—fast medical treatment is your pet's best chance for survival.

Poisoning

"Excuse me a minute," said Mistletoe's owner suddenly, in the middle of a telephone conversation we were having. "I think Mistletoe is eating my vitamin pills."

My friend's vitamins didn't affect Mistletoe one way or the other, but the incident serves to illustrate the point that cats will sometimes eat stuff they shouldn't. It's hard to second-guess a cat; I once had one that liked to lick photographs—glossies, not those with matte finish. I had to remember not to leave snapshots around. An occasional cat will lick the glue from the moisten-and-seal type of paper tape. If you catch your cat doing this, you'll have to remember to keep anything with this tape loose on it out of reach. If it ate a lot of this glue, it might get sick.

Fortunately, it is quite unusual for cats to actually ingest a poison directly. However, they do sometimes get toxins on their feet or fur and then become sick when they lick the stuff off. A cat's compulsive dedication to cleanliness may be its undoing. A kitten is especially susceptible to poisonous substances.

Insecticides and roach or rat killers probably account for most cat poison cases. It's best not to put any toxins around —get a good exterminator who uses sprays that won't harm pets. Medicines, bleach, powerful cleaners, polishes, paint, and other familiar household products are also dangerous to cats. Be sure to rinse the tub and sink after scrubbing it with a cleanser, and keep your cat off a freshly waxed floor until it dries. Cats can even be poisoned from nibbling crayons. House plants can also be harmful (see below).

Fortunately, cats are equipped with an efficient regurgitating apparatus that helps them get rid of toxic substances fast. Even so, a cat can become ill—or dead!—if lethal material is absorbed into the bloodstream.

Symptoms of poisoning are vomiting, hard breathing, salivation, crying, intense abdominal pain, trembling, perhaps convulsions. Coughing and diarrhea may also be present. As you can imagine, poisoning is serious, so you have to act fast.

The first thing you must do—instantly—is find the cause. It's crucial that you know what your pet swallowed. Then telephone your veterinarian quickly and follow his or her directions. Keep cool; your pet's life depends on you. If you can't get immediate veterinary advice, telephone your local poison control center and ask what to do. Then, after you have given appropriate first aid, get your cat to a vet as soon as possible.

If you can't get immediate first-aid advice from a veterinarian or poison control center, then you must act on your own, because seconds count.

If you know what poison your animal has ingested, look on the bottle or container for directions—many products tell you what to do. The procedure for a cat is the same as for a human being.

However, if the bottle does not advise you, then you have to know whether to induce vomiting or whether to give something to neutralize the poison instead. This is an important distinction.

You should induce vomiting if the substance is nonacid or nonalkali. Nonacid and nonalkali substances include medicines, insecticide or rat killer, paint, dye, crayons, indelible markers, and alcohol.

The most effective emetic is syrup of ipecac; give the pediatric dose suggested on the bottle. Another good emetic is hydrogen peroxide (3 percent solution, not the kind for bleaching hair) mixed with an equal amount of water. If you haven't got peroxide, powdered mustard—one tablespoon in a cup of warm water—will do. Lacking that, mix a teaspoon of salt in a cup of warm water. Whatever emetic you use, administer a teaspoon at a time until the cat vomits. Then stop giving the emetic and get your cat, along with the vomitus, to a veterinarian.

While it's unlikely that your indoor cat will have access to ethylene glycol (antifreeze), you should know that this is one really lethal substance that cats adore. There have been cases of cats crawling into the underpinnings of cars to get at any antifreeze that has dripped or spilled from the radiator. A cat poisoned with this stuff will be drowsy and staggering; its rear quarters may be paralyzed. You should induce vomiting at once and get it to a veterinarian quickly.

If you discover your cat has just gotten antifreeze on its fur but fortunately hasn't licked it off yet, immediately wash every drop of the substance off thoroughly with soap and water. Antifreeze is big trouble.

You should not induce vomiting if the cat has swallowed an acid or alkali substance. Acid and alkali substances include polishes, cleaners, bleach, detergents, wax, paint remover and thinner, gasoline, kerosene, and lye. It would have to be an eccentric cat to eat any of these, even out of curiosity, but a fastidious animal that got any on its paws or coat could conceivably ingest enough to hurt it seriously. You should get milk of magnesia, egg white, or plain milk down its throat, and flush its mouth out with a lot of water. Then rush your pet to a veterinarian.

It is admittedly hard to get anything down the throat of a struggling cat in the throes of abdominal cramps, but you have to do it, whether you are trying to induce vomiting or neutralize what's in its stomach. The recommended method is to wrap the cat firmly in a towel so it can't struggle, hold its head up at a 45-degree angle, pull the corner of its mouth out, and pour in small amounts of the liquid. If the animal doesn't swallow, keep holding its head at the angle and tap its nose gently with your finger or blow on its nose.

If you're pretty sure your pet is poisoned but you can't discover the cause quickly, don't waste time searching the house—rush the cat to the vet. It might help if you can get a couple of teaspoons of powered activated charcoal (mixed with a little milk) down its throat to absorb the poison, whatever it is. You might keep ipecac syrup and powdered activated charcoal (available at drugstores) in your medicine cabinet or first-aid kit.

It's unlikely you'll ever have a poisoned cat on your hands, but it's useful to know what to do just in case.

House plants

I've put house plants in a special category, because my experience with cats has been that your pet is far more likely to nibble on your plants than to have harmful contact with poisonous household products. (For a discussion of the problem of house plant-eating, from the point of view of protecting your plants, see Chapter Eight.)

Fortunately, when cats eat plant leaves, they usually vomit, which gets rid of toxins before they can do much damage. You can tell when your cat has been nibbling plants because you can see the leaves when you clean up the vomit. Olivia sometimes takes a mouthful of my false aralia when I'm not looking and throws it up, and when I wipe up after her, I notice the chewed-up leaves.

But while house-plant poisoning is relatively rare among cats, some plants would be really bad news to your cat if it ate them, and therefore they should be considered a safety hazard. Many plants that are poisonous to animals are out-door types such as oleander, wisteria, lily of the valley, loco-weed—you wouldn't be likely to have them growing in your house. But you might very well have the following:

Dieffenbachia has an almost instant effect on a cat that eats it—the animal will writhe in pain and foam at the mouth. Induce vomiting immediately (see above), and then rush it to a veterinarian.

Philodendron poisoning is slow-acting. The cat will be-come listless, lose its appetite, and vomit frequently. If your cat shows these symptoms and you have a philodendron, check the plant for nibbled leaves, and if you find any, get rid of the plant at once and take your pet to the veteri-narian.

Berries can be lethal, and for this reason I can't have bit-tersweet branches in the fall, or Christmas cherry, holly, or mistletoe. I figure it's not fair to my pets to take a chance with their lives or health for the sake of decoration.

Poinsettia, English ivy, daffodil, caladium, and *laurel* leaves can make cats extremely sick.

Those marvelous bouquets of bright-colored *dried flowers* are a problem because they're irresistible to cats and the dyes are toxic.

A cat with house-plant poisoning should be made to vomit (see above) and then taken to a veterinarian.

Safe plants, by the way, include Swedish ivy, coleus, Afri-can violets, spider plants, ferns, and palms.

Swallowed foreign objects

Before I knew that cats could get stomach or intestinal ob-structions or severed intestines from Christmas tree tinsel, I used to notice that they threw it up all over the house. Fortunately, I gave up tinsel years ago, before anybody was harmed.

I'm very careful to keep the lid tight on my sewing basket —not just to prevent the cats from stealing spools to play with, but because a swallowed needle or pin can kill a cat.

Rubber bands, cellophane, foil, thread, string, and ribbon are a problem because cats love to play with them, and if swallowed, these homely necessities can cause havoc with a cat's insides. Watch what you toss in the garbage—the string from a roast will attract a cat like a magnet. Sometimes rubber bands, string, and the like just pass on through, but if they ball up in the stomach or intestinal tract, they can cause serious obstruction. If you see your pet eating any of these objects, remove it at once unless some of it is already swallowed. If you know only a little has been swallowed, you can pull it out—very gently—but if a lot has already gone down, don't. Especially if you see one end of the string under the tongue and the rest disappears down the throat, leave it alone. You risk pulling the animal's innards out with it. Telephone your veterinarian for instructions—he or she may advise inducing vomiting, or giving a laxative, or more drastic medical treatment in the office.

All my cats love to watch me wrap presents—the rustle of the paper, the folding, the tying of ribbon must be incredibly fascinating to them. They range themselves where they can get a good view and follow every motion. They also wait for me to turn away for a second so they can grab snippets of ribbon and run off with them. They especially love the crinkly paper ribbon that curls so nicely. Many times I've caught Gina under a table chomping away on a wet, limp few inches of paper ribbon, and she always seems so disappointed when I take it away from her.

I heard of a pet that choked on a rubber band, not in but *around* its throat. A child had thoughtlessly put a slim rubber band around the kitten's throat under its fur and forgotten about it. Nobody noticed. As the poor animal grew, the band tightened and cut into its neck. The cat was practically garroted before the idiot adults in that family noticed anything wrong.

An animal that's choking on a swallowed object is another matter. It will paw at its mouth, gag, and drool. Quickly hold it upside down by the hind legs and shake it slightly to make it cough. Even if the object comes out, it's wise to take the cat to a veterinarian to be sure it's all out and there's no damage to the throat. If the object is already in the esophagus, the cat may vomit, retch, cough, and gulp repeatedly. It needs fast medical help.

Other objects to avoid letting your cat have access to are the three B's—buttons, beads, and bells—which can get stuck in its throat and choke it. A lot of toys for cats are thoughtlessly made with these on them, so remove them before you give such a toy to your cat. There is no evidence that a cat enjoys the tinkle of the bell on a catnip mouse, so you're not depriving it of anything.

Broken glass should of course be swept up thoroughly, because it's possible a cat could step on a tiny fragment that sticks to its paw and then lick it off. Chances are the cat would spit out a glass splinter rather than swallow it, but could cut its tongue or mouth. Broken glass could also of course cut its paw.

Heat stroke

Every year, especially in summer, untold numbers of cats suffer and die in parked cars that overheat and become deathtraps. People think that if they leave the windows open an inch at the top, this provides enough ventilation and cooling for a living creature inside. But a parked car in hot weather can heat up to well over 100 degrees, even in the shade—and, also, the shade you left the car in can turn into glaring sunshine as the day progresses. Even in cold weather, a car in the sun can heat up enough to kill a cat inside. (See *Traveling with a cat*, Appendix.)

Unfortunately, most cats that suffer heat stroke do not survive. But in the event that you find a cat in an overheated car still alive but collapsed, panting, with a rapid pulse and a staring expression, possibly vomiting, you have to bring its temperature down immediately.

Immerse it in cold water or sponge it all over, and put ice packs on its head. Place it on the seat of a car with the windows open and continue to sponge it while someone drives it to a veterinarian as fast as possible.

Burns

In the kitchen, one of the most likely places your cat will be is right where you're about to step. Not only might you crush one of its paws, you could fall yourself, and you might spill hot water or grease or food onto your pet and yourself.

An iron, particularly a steam iron, is also a danger to a cat, especially because it has the additional attraction of a dangling cord.

Burn treatment for your cat will depend on the degree of the burn. If the animal's skin is red and painful, the hair singed but still attached, it is a first-degree burn. Cover the burn with a sterile cloth and take your pet to the veterinarian. The doctor will probably shave the fur in order to see the extent of the burn. Since it's impossible to see how much of the skin is burned under the fur, the animal may be more seriously hurt than you think.

A slight burn on the footpads can be given emergency treatment with a paste you make of baking soda and cool water. The cat will of course lick this off unless you put a sterile bandage on the paw to cover the burn, and you'll have a problem keeping the cat from trying to pull off the bandage. But if the burn is very minor and you know for certain that no other part of the body is burned, the animal probably doesn't need further medical treatment. Of course, a bad burn on the footpad needs medical attention.

Second-degree burns are swollen and the skin may slough off. In third-degree burns, the skin is blackened or maybe whitish, the hair falls out, and there may be less pain because the nerve ends are destroyed. Second- and third-degree burns call for emergency treatment for shock, as well as medical attention for the burns.

When a cat goes into shock, its body is cold, its gums are white, it appears unconscious, and its breathing is shallow. Wrap the cat warmly in blankets, with its head lower than its body. Rush it to the vet. Shock is serious, a killer.

Burns by electrical wiring are also possible if your cat chews on a lamp cord or the like. Kittens especially have to be protected from this because, to them, electrical cords are attractive playthings. In fact, if you have a playful cat or kitten, it's best to disconnect electrical appliances when you're not using them. (The telephone cord, by the way, is not a problem; it could shock only if the bell were ringing when the cat bit through the cord, and even then the voltage is minimal.)

If you find your animal has bitten through an electrical cord and is unable to let go of it, or is unconscious and still attached to the cord, unplug the appliance before you pick up the animal, or else knock the animal away from the cord with a stick—otherwise you might get a shock yourself.

N.B. If your cat sleeps on your electric blanket or heating pad, be sure there is lots of protective material between it and your cat—especially if the animal kneads it.

If your pet does chew on an electrical cord and suffers a shock, the burns on its lips and mouth are usually minor and are no indication of the severity of the damage. The big

problem is the likelihood of pulmonary edema. Treat your
pet for shock and get it to the vet, even if it is breathing, its
heart is beating, and it looks okay.

If the shocked cat stops breathing, you must give it
mouth-to-mouth resuscitation—no kidding. Wrap the cat
warmly in blankets, put it on its side, and clean its mouth of
any obstruction, blood, or mucus. Inhale, put your mouth
firmly over its muzzle, and exhale gently and slowly. Remove your mouth, then repeat in about five seconds. Keep
this up until the cat is breathing, then get it to a veterinarian.

Smoke inhalation may also cause pulmonary edema, by
the way. If your cat is overcome by smoke, it is in great danger even if it isn't burned. Give it mouth-to-mouth resuscitation—on the way to the veterinarian.

Hiding places

There's truth in that old saw, "Curiosity killed the cat." Cats
are indeed curious creatures, and sometimes this quality can
get them into trouble, even in a house or apartment. Not
only do they have to investigate every unlikely place, but
they can squeeze themselves into tiny spaces or scale amazing heights. It's always wise to be continually aware of this.
A friend of mine once adopted a kitten from a shelter, and
phoned me an hour later saying that it had disappeared
while she'd gone to the store for ten minutes to buy kitten
food. It was only when I thought of removing the cover
from the front of the refrigerator base that we found the
tiny thing, crouched in under all the pipes. Don't ask me
how it got in there.

The trouble with cats' hiding places is the cats' frequently
poor judgment in selecting them. While it won't hurt puss to
be accidentally shut in a closet or drawer for a while,
cats have also been known to crawl into unlit ovens,

dishwashers, clothes washers, dryers (nice and warm, right?), and even refrigerators. Also, children have put cats into these appliances. I need not dwell on this—you get the picture.

It's a rare cat owner who hasn't had the experience of having his or her cat disappear and reappear mysteriously. You've called and called, searched every inch of the house to no avail, and then you turn around to find your pet sitting in the middle of the floor gazing at you innocently, as if to say, "What's all the fuss about? I was here all the time."

Most of us check our cat's whereabouts automatically before leaving the house, just to be sure it's not shut in a closet somewhere. Poor Fred once spent a day in my clothes closet, and not only was glad to be released when I came home but scolded me about it for nearly an hour.

I even heard a story about a man who left for work one morning and had gotten halfway down his block when an unusual craving for a drink of water caused him to go back home. When he opened the refrigerator door to get out the bottle of ice water he kept there, he discovered his new kitten shivering inside. He must have been half asleep when he got out the orange juice and simply didn't notice his cat jumping in. Luckily for the cat, it was found before it froze to death.

Cats have a habit of hiding the minute there's the least bit of commotion. This is okay when you are visited by a bevy of children or repairmen or other noisemakers; the cat will simply reappear when the coast is clear. Some cats hide all day during a street fair or on the Fourth of July in a noisy neighborhood. I've heard of cats that hide during electrical storms.

The problem comes when your cat disappears at a time when it is important for you to know where it is—say, when you're about to depart on a trip, or you're closing up a summer place for the winter. I heard of one clever man who, after packing for a trip, missed his cat, searched everywhere, and finally found it by turning off all the lights in the house and searching with a flashlight. Sure enough, the cat was watching all the activity from behind the books on a shelf and could only be seen when the beam of the flashlight picked up the gleam of its eyes.

I think it's important for an owner to be privy to all the cat's haunts, in case of fire or some other emergency. You might have to locate your cat in a hurry for its own good. If you have to grab it quickly, pop it in its carrying case, and get out of the house, you don't want to lose time looking for it. Also, remember that a sick or injured cat will often hide.

A cat does need its hiding places, but when there's no emergency, you don't have to disturb it when you discover it in one. Just look casually and go away—or even pretend you don't see it, if you want. When Olivia, for instance, is in her hiding place at the back of a closet shelf, I just ignore her and remember to leave the closet door open so she can get out when she wants. But if I ever missed her and needed to know in a hurry where she might be, I'd know where to look.

Speaking of Olivia's hiding place, she gets very upset if I completely close the door to that closet, even if she is not in it. She may not want to go to her spot on the shelf at that moment, but she wants access to it. She'll cry at the door till I open it, then run in the closet, stop, and come right out again. But she plainly wants the door left open.

Cats are funny about closed doors anyway. The minute you shut a door, they want to be on the other side of it. On the rare occasions when I have had guests who preferred that the cats not be around them, I've shut my cats in the bedroom. They cluster at the closed door and scratch and mew. And yet, many evenings you'll find them all snoring away on my bed of their own accord. What they object to is not being in the bedroom itself, but the closed door.

Don't worry, by the way, if your pet likes to hide under

From a cat's point of view, an ideal, and safe, place to sit, with a screened window to look out, a curtain to peek around.

No cat in its right mind can resist plants with dangling fronds.

Who would ever think this innocent, adorable, enchanting creature could get into mischief?

Let's just hope this busy imp doesn't swallow any of that thread.

Common city scene: a watchful little face in a window.

Perhaps this cat is saying to itself, "They should be along any minute now..."

the bedspread. Cats are notorious for that. They won't smother—they'll come out when they need more air. Lots of fresh-air-fiend people who sleep with their windows open all winter report that their cats crawl way down under the covers at their feet and sleep there all night.

The one thing you cannot predict or avoid is occasionally stepping on your cat. They simply will get under our feet. Owners have accidentally broken their pets' paws, but in all probability you'll only hurt it. The cat will let out a loud shriek, you'll be badly startled, the cat will run away and hide or glower at you accusingly from a distance. When that happens, simply apologize, and soothe your pet. Make a big sympathetic fuss. I believe cats know when you didn't intend to hurt them, and a little comforting goes a long way. They'll quickly forgive you.

Much of knowing how to protect your indoor pet from dangers in the house is simply a matter of using common sense and empathy. You don't need me to tell you, for example, that an electric fan could break a cat's paw if the animal tried to play with the whirling blades, so you should get one with narrow mesh covering. If your cat is one of those geniuses who figures out how to turn doorknobs (some can do this!), and you have seen it fiddle with the knobs on the gas stove, be sure the handles of the burners are too tight for the animal to turn on, or keep it out of the kitchen when you're not there.

There is no way you can protect your cat from every conceivable accident, any more than you can protect your child or yourself. The point is that if you're aware of the common serious dangers and take measures against them, the rest probably won't happen. The longevity of the well-cared-for indoor cat attests to this. An attentive and caring owner of an indoor cat will probably never have to contend with most of the emergencies described in this chapter, but it's better to know how to avoid or deal with them, just in case.

chapter seven

General Health:
Illnesses, Vaccinations,
Neutering

An important characteristic of the indoor cat is that its life expectancy is twelve to fifteen or more years, as opposed to the overall average for all cats of eleven years. The cat that has a home but is allowed to roam lives an estimated average of two years—and the homeless cat averages a year or less.

A well-cared-for indoor cat is seldom sick. Nevertheless, it is probably impossible for any cat to live its entire life without ever coming down with at least a few of the many ailments of catdom. While this book is not intended as a medical handbook on all feline diseases, I do hope to help you identify and deal with the most likely ones your indoor cat could conceivably develop. Most important, you can learn how to prevent some of them.

I've included neutering at the end of this discussion. While it's not an illness, neutering is a medical procedure, and it prevents more than pregnancy, heat (estrus), and spraying. Neutering is essential for the emotional well-being of the indoor cat, since confinement would exaggerate the stress of unrequited sexual urges. Neutering your cat will preserve your sanity, too, as anyone who has ever tried to live with an unneutered indoor cat will tell you. And neutering offers an especially great advantage to a female cat. She will be far less prone to breast cancer and to disorders of the reproductive system so common among unspayed females.

Symptoms of illness

Your cat can't come to you and say, "Gee, I feel terrible," but when you know your pet, you can recognize when it is sick. As a sentient vertebrate, just like us, a cat acts much as we do when we're ill.

But sometimes a cat, like a child, will exhibit what seems to be an illness symptom but actually means nothing serious. This can be confusing until you learn to differentiate. For example, one morning your cat throws up its breakfast. If it then goes about its business normally, and keeps its food down thereafter, you can probably safely assume it simply had a hair ball, its food didn't agree with it or was too cold, or something scared it. You can just watch your pet more carefully than usual to be sure nothing further develops. My cat Fred is a nervous eater—he has to have absolute peace and quiet while he eats. Just let the doorbell ring suddenly, and up will come his meal. He's startled, but not sick. *But* if Fred were to vomit several times over, say, a day and a half, I'd know something was wrong with him that needed medical attention.

Or, let's say you pick up your pet and notice it seems hot, and upon taking its temperature, you discover it is running 102.5°. Veterinarians differ on what a cat's normal temperature is, but the range seems to be 100° to 102.5°, so your cat is borderline. Has it been romping around; has it had a quarrel with one of its housemates; is the house or apart-

ment overheated? A cat can get an elevated temperature
from hot weather, exercise, or excitement. If there are no
other symptoms, you don't have to be concerned—just keep
an eye on your pet, especially if it's an older cat.

Another example might be if you were stroking your cat
one day and its coat seemed dull to you. A dry, dull coat can
be an illness symptom, but if the animal seems otherwise
healthy, it probably only needs a dietary supplement—and
regular brushing.

I once got a scare from a little cat of ours named Charlie.
I came into the kitchen and found him prostrate on his
stomach on the floor, breathing heavily. In a panic, I lifted
him gently and tried to get him to stand on his legs, but
they collapsed under him again. And as I supported him I
noticed that his stomach seemed bloated. I stood up, trying
to decide whether to telephone our veterinarian or rush
Charlie to the animal hospital emergency room, and then I
noticed something. Almost an entire platter of spaghetti
with clam sauce that had been on the counter had disappeared. Charlie wasn't suffering from some terrible neuro-
logical disorder—he'd simply OD'd on spaghetti, and his
skinny adolescent legs wouldn't support his overloaded
stomach.

Here's a checklist of symptoms that can indicate trouble,
especially if more than one is present:
   Loss of appetite
   Excessive thirst
   Lethargy, depression
   Weakness
   Failure to clean itself
   Persistent hiding (a sick cat may seek seclusion)
   Persistent or violent vomiting
   Diarrhea, especially bloody
   Frequent urination; blood in urine
   Straining and inability to urinate or defecate

Very pale gums and tongue
Dull coat; hair falling out in patches
Dehydration (skin remains up when you pinch it)
Frantic scratching or biting the skin
Head shaking; pawing at its ears
Rapid or slow breathing
Persistent coughing
Trembling
Temperature below 100° or above 102.5° (For how to
    take a cat's temperature, see below.)

Each of the above can be a symptom of any one of many
cat disorders. A single symptom such as frequent, bloody
urination needs medical treatment without delay. However,
a pair of symptoms such as loss of appetite and hiding could
just mean your cat is upset—perhaps by some change in
household members or routine. You yourself can learn to
distinguish between serious and minor symptoms, but only a
veterinarian can diagnose those that are significant, discover
related symptoms, and prescribe treatment for your pet.

Don't dose your cat yourself with human medicine. Don't
give it a shot of whiskey or brandy. Above all, *don't give it
aspirin*—it will kill your cat. And don't give it medicine left
over from the time it had a similar illness two years ago, either.

Even though you need a vet to diagnose and prescribe
when your cat is really ill, you play the key role because you
will be the first to notice when it needs that medical help.
Learn to know your cat's body well. Regularly, when you're
petting it, get in the habit of looking in its ears, eyes, and
mouth and under its tail. Feel its sides and belly, check its
footpads. An alert owner who picks up anomalies and symptoms early can avoid many serious feline health problems—
even save the pet's life by prompt discovery. (You'll have
fewer and lower veterinary bills, too.)

Vaccinations

Fortunately, you can have your cat immunized against several of the killers among cat diseases. It's essential to have even a totally indoor cat given these vaccinations. The diseases are highly contagious, and while the viruses are not airborne to the extent that they can come in a window, you can bring them in from the outside on your clothing. Some veterinarians believe that indoor cats especially need these shots because, by not ever being exposed to the disease agents, the animals have no chance to build up antibodies on their own. Therefore, should an unvaccinated indoor cat come in contact with the viruses, it has no defenses.

The first inoculation your pet should receive is the FVRCP vaccine, which stands for Feline Virus Rhinotracheitis Calici Panleukopenia.

Rhinotracheitis is a severe coldlike disease that attacks the animal's nose, throat, and eyes. Its onset is characterized by a discharge from the nose and eyes, difficult breathing, inflamed throat, coughing, and, as might be expected, loss of appetite.

Calici is similar to rhinotracheitis, with additional discharge from the mouth. It may develop into pneumonia.

Panleukopenia—also known as distemper, cat fever, and feline infectious enteritis—causes a cat to be lethargic and feverish, with persistent vomiting and bloody, watery diarrhea. The animal may also drool. In the unfortunate event that your pet gets this monstrous feline disease, it will quickly spread to any other unvaccinated cats you have. The virus is resistant to disinfectant and will remain in the house for as long as a year. An owner who loses a cat to panleukopenia should not bring in another for at least a month—and then only an already well-vaccinated cat.

A cat should receive its initial FVRCP shot at eight weeks

of age, the second at eleven weeks, and a third at fourteen weeks, with an annual booster thereafter.

By the way, a kitten may show mild respiratory symptoms after receiving the FVRCP vaccine. Bear in mind that these symptoms are infinitely less dangerous to the kitten than the full-blown disease, and the signs will pass in two or three days. As long as the kitten continues to eat and drink, there is no cause to worry.

If you should have a cat with any of the above three diseases, you shouldn't visit anyone who has a cat during the time yours is ill.

You can also have your cat protected against *pneumonitis*, a relatively mild respiratory disease characterized by a discharge from highly inflamed eyes, a nasal discharge, and some difficulty in breathing. While pneumonitis generally runs its course in three to five days, you might still want to get your cat vaccinated against it. A pneumonitis shot can be given at twelve weeks, another at nine months, and an annual booster thereafter.

Veterinarians differ somewhat on the type and schedule of vaccinations they prefer, so follow the schedule yours recommends. However, there's a single vaccine for all four of the above diseases that's new at this writing; so far, it's best to avoid this because there have been significant reports of bad reactions.

Your cat can also be vaccinated against *rabies*. If you take your pet with you to the country where it might get outdoors and come into contact with a rabid animal, it's wise to give it this protection. Also, if you have a cat with an unsocial disposition, which could conceivably bite a visitor, you yourself might need the legal protection of being able to prove that your pet has been inoculated against rabies. And if you plan to take your cat abroad with you, it must be inoculated against rabies in order to enter certain countries.

Check with the consulate of each country you plan to visit. (Don't expect your veterinarian to know the requirements of every country.)

Urolithiasis (urinary disorders)

What happens in cases of cystitis, cystic calculi, and urethral calculi is that the crystalline salts and protein material in a cat's urine form into sandlike granules or even stones that irritate or block the urinary passages. The cause of this is unknown. Bacteria, viruses, stress, diet, low water intake, and lack of exercise have all been suspected. Another very likely cause is an unclean litter box that a cat is reluctant to use—it will retain its urine on purpose. Foods high in ash (mineral) content have been blamed for urolithiasis, too, but whether they cause or only aggravate the condition is unknown.

Male cats, because of the naturally narrow shape of their urethras, are more prone to urolithiasis than females. Indoor cats are perhaps more susceptible than others because of lack of exercise, especially if they are obese. And some cats just seem more predisposed than others. If you're buying or adopting a male kitten whose father is known, you might inquire about the father's history in this department, since a particularly narrow urethra might be inherited. If you're forewarned about any possibility of urinary difficulties, you can be especially vigilant for trouble signs as the kitten grows older.

Any time a cat breaks litter-box training, urolithiasis should be suspected. The first symptoms in females may be little dribbles of bloody urine around the house—in the bathtub, on the kitchen floor, wherever. Or you may notice your pet, especially a male, making frequent trips to the litter box and staying in it for long periods, straining to urinate. A male cat may lick its penis agitatedly. The animal may lose its appetite, or might eat eagerly and then vomit. It may become careless about its grooming.

Be sure not to confuse the symptoms of urolithiasis with those of constipation. Check to see if there is stool in the litter box; the vet will need to know.

Whatever the cause, urolithiasis is serious and requires fast professional treatment. A urinary blockage can kill a cat in forty-eight to seventy-two hours. The five stages of urolithiasis are: 1) difficulty in urinating, 2) refusal to eat, 3) vomiting, 4) coma, and 5) death, so don't neglect the symptoms. *Prompt medical attention is essential.*

Feline leukemia and other cancers

What can I tell you about feline leukemia, this all-too-common, serious, and contagious viral disease of cats? Feline leukemia (lymphosarcoma) is a cancerous disease of the white blood cells caused by the feline leukemia virus (FeLV). It is diagnosed by a blood test. And at this point, there is no cure.

Symptoms of the disease could include loss of appetite, pale gums, weight loss, labored breathing, chronic vomiting, chronic diarrhea, weakness, and high susceptibility to infections and vague illnesses. If your cat has these symptoms, you should have it tested for feline leukemia.

If the cat tests out positive, there are treatments for some forms of the disease, and you should get supportive treatment for the cat. Also, although the disease is not curable, the animal could go into remission from time to time. Just make it as comfortable as possible and keep it isolated from other cats. Disinfect everything the sick cat has used or come in contact with, if possible, to protect your other cats. As your pet deteriorates, it is a kindness eventually to have it euthanized, since you can be sure in the later stages it is not enjoying its life.

Once you know you have a cat with feline leukemia, you should have all your other cats tested. If any of your other cats test positive and the rest are negative, you should separate the positive ones from the others, even if the positive cats seem well. They may not necessarily become sick, but they are carriers. A cat can carry the FeLV and never actually contract the disease, or may carry it for months or even years before becoming sick, but will surely pass it along to susceptible negative cats.

If all your cats show a positive reaction to the FeLV test, there's nothing you can do—they may all get sick, or they may live a relatively normal life-span. But you should not bring in a new cat that is negative.

The FeLV must be transferred from cat to cat by direct contact—licking, eating from the same bowl, using the same litter box, biting. The virus is not airborne, and you can't carry it on your clothing.

If you have a single cat that dies of feline leukemia, throw out its bowl, bed, toys, and litter box, and wait a month before you get another cat.

There is no evidence that FeLV is contagious to human beings.

Other forms of cancer cats get include skin cancer, bone cancer, cancer of the digestive system, and breast cancer (more common in unspayed females). Treatment is about the same as among human beings: surgery, drugs, and/or radiation, which sometimes cures the cat, sometimes not.

Internal parasites (worms)

Various types of parasites are common in cats because they can come from so many different sources. Every kitten, no matter where you got it—from a private home, shelter, pet shop, or breeder—should have one or more stool examinations. Any cat adopted from the street probably has parasites. Any cat that has fleas most likely has internal parasites as well. A house cat that is given raw meat or fish can get internal parasites.

The thing to remember is that each type of parasite is different, and there is no medicine that works for all. Your cat might have *tapeworm, ascarids,* or *coccidia.* Cats in the southern parts of the United States might even have *hookworms.* That's why your cat's stool sample must be examined by a veterinarian so the particular parasite can be identified and the right medicine in the proper dosage prescribed. Sometimes parasites will not show up in a single stool sample, and it's necessary to have several samples checked before the vet can spot the worms or their eggs. Any worm medicine is, of course, poison, and a poison capable of killing worms can also kill a cat if misused.

N.B. Never dose your cat with any of the commercial worm medicines you can buy in pet shops, five-and-tens, supermarkets, and the like.

Symptoms of internal parasites are lethargy, weight loss, bloated stomach, diarrhea, and a dull, coarse coat. The animal may lose its appetite—or become voracious. It may sometimes vomit worms. Coughing and runny eyes are not uncommon.

Tapeworms look like little rice kernels that may be moving around (these are pieces of the worm). You can often see them in the animal's stool or around the anus. Fleas are the intermediate hosts of tapeworms.

Ascarids or roundworms are four to six inches long, and in severe cases a cat may vomit them up—a disgusting sight you're not likely to forget. Ascarid eggs are hard to see except under a microscope because they are so tiny.

Tapeworms and ascarids are fairly easy to get rid of with proper medicine given on schedule.

Coccidia on the other hand can be a serious parasite. A cat with coccidia will seem sick—emaciated and anemic, depressed, dehydrated, and with diarrhea, abdominal pain, nasal and eye discharge. An animal contracts coccidia from eating raw meat, mice, or birds, or from unsanitary quarters where it comes in contact with infected feces. If you bail a cat out of a dirty pet shop or animal shelter, or take one in from the street (and we all are likely to do this at some time or other), be sure to have it checked right away by a veterinarian, and isolate it from other cats until you're sure it's okay.

One strain of coccidia causes toxoplasmosis. The cat will lose its appetite, cough, have labored breathing and fever. It needs medical treatment. The only way a healthy indoor cat is likely to get toxoplasmosis is from raw meat. (That's why I feel raw meat should be a diet no-no, always.) Don't forget, raw meat includes mice as well as steak tartare.

Conceivably, if a healthy indoor cat used the same litter box with an infected cat, it could get the parasite from contact with the feces of the infected cat—but the feces would have to be at least forty-eight hours old, and a careful cat owner is not likely to let feces remain in a litter box that long.

We once rescued an abandoned cat at a summer resort—a typical place to find a discarded animal at the end of summer, thanks to callous and stupid people. This cat was sitting in a garbage can trying to eat watermelon rind. She was on her last legs, not only with a respiratory infection but all three types of internal parasites. It's a credit to modern veterinary medicine—and her own will to survive, plus our care —that she lived. Today, Kismet is a healthy, beautiful pet in a good home in Brooklyn.

External parasites

When we lived where my cats had access to the city garden, they routinely wore flea collars every summer, and even then we sometimes had to do further battle with tapeworms. Since the cats have lived totally indoors, they haven't had either fleas or tapes—even though the dog, who is of course walked regularly on the streets, has occasionally suffered from a flea or two.

Nevertheless, owners of indoor cats sometimes do find their pets mysteriously afflicted with these devilish parasites, which may get in the house somehow. And many people who take their pets with them on vacations or on weekends in the country have had to cope with one or another type of parasite.

Fleas are little fast-moving black insects found particularly on the cat's head, around the neck, and at the base of the back near the tail. Symptoms of fleas are of course furious scratching and biting the skin. If you brush the cat's fur the wrong way and look, you can often see the parasites themselves, or the black specks of dried blood they leave.

Fleas, because they suck the animal's blood, can so debilitate an adult cat that it becomes anemic and a good candidate to succumb to the first virus it meets. A kitten can be killed by fleas. My son once took in a half-dead, very tiny, homeless kitten, and with his fingers removed and killed some sixty fleas that were eating the little creature alive. He undoubtedly saved its life. (That kitten grew up to be big, good-natured Thompson Jones.)

Probably the best prevention of fleas is the controversial flea collar. Because of the poisonous chemicals in it, you should be cautious when you put one on your pet—follow the directions to the letter. Some vets recommend airing a flea collar for two or three days after you take it out of its package, before putting it on your cat. Here are some good rules to follow concerning flea collars:

1. Never put a flea collar on a kitten.
2. Don't put a dog flea collar on a cat.
3. Don't put the collar on hanging loosely; on the other

hand, it mustn't be too tight either—you should be able to easily slip your finger between the collar and the cat's neck.

4. Cut off any excess (and throw it away where your pet won't find it and play with it) so the animal can't chew the end.

5. Examine your cat's neck regularly for signs of redness or irritation, and if this occurs, remove the collar at once.

6. Never use a flea collar in combination with other remedies such as flea powder or dip.

7. Be extremely careful if you put a flea collar on a Persian or other long-haired cat. For unknown reasons, many long-haired cats develop systemic toxicity from flea collars.

If your cat sleeps on your pillow, you might want to take the collar off at night and put it back on the cat in the morning, so your face won't come in contact with the collar over several hours at a time.

By the way, I have found those flea medallions you can attach to cats' regular collars to be ineffectual.

There is a growing theory—with some evidence—that the vitamin B_1 in Brewers' yeast prevents fleas on a cat. Since Brewers' yeast is good for a cat anyway, there's no harm in giving this idea a try during the flea season, especially if you have dogs that could bring fleas into the house from the outdoors. You apparently have to let the B_1 build up in the cat's system, so begin the administration of ½ to 1 teaspoon of yeast in the cat's food daily a month ahead of the flea season.

Frequent, thorough brushing and combing of your pet's coat will help get rid of parasites and their eggs. Stand the cat on a newspaper to catch those that drop off (and burn the paper afterward). Unless the cat is wearing a flea collar, this would be a good time to flea-powder it. Stroke the fur the wrong way so the powder can go clear to the skin—don't just sprinkle it on the surface of the fur.

If your cat gets a bad infestation of fleas, you may have to bathe it in a medicated dip. Put cotton in its ears, a drop of mineral oil in each eye, and follow directions on the bottle. Be sure to rinse and dry the animal thoroughly (see *Bathing a cat*, in Chapter Five). Remember that, just as the medicine that kills internal parasites is poison, the agents that kill off external parasites are also poisons. Dips, collars, sprays, powders—all poisons, so use accordingly. *And be sure not to use any in combination.*

Never use a medicated dip on a kitten. You can often get rid of fleas on a kitten, however, by just bathing it in mild soap and water. Be sure to put cotton in its ears, a drop of mineral oil in each eye, rinse thoroughly, and keep the animal especially warm while you dry it completely.

Fleas are the devil to get rid of if your house or apartment becomes infested. You may have to vacuum clean every inch, especially the rugs and upholstery, and then get an exterminator to come in and do a real job.

Don't forget that any animal that has fleas will most likely have tapeworm too. Have your pet tested by the veterinarian and give it worm medicine if necessary, after you've defleaed it.

Ticks are rare on cats, but in a heavy tick season may get in a house and attach themselves to cats. Flea collars will give some protection against them. If your cat does get ticks, it's necessary to take it to a veterinarian to have them removed because they bury their heads in the animal's skin, and it's no good just to pull off a tick, leaving its head still in the cat to become infected.

Lice are tiny pinheads, hard to see. They don't move around but also bury themselves in the animal's skin. A cat will often bite its skin to relieve the itch. Flea powders or sprays will usually get rid of lice.

Mites, which include *sarcoptic mange*, cause itching and discomfort, and in addition, the cat's hair falls out, revealing inflammation, pimples, lesions, and scabs on the skin. A veterinarian has to examine a scraping of the animal's skin under a microscope to identify and prescribe for mites. Don't bathe or dip the animal yourself.

Far and away the most common type of mite is the *ear mite*, which causes a black discharge in the animal's ears. The cat shakes its head and scratches and paws at its ears. Ear mites, once identified by a veterinarian, can be successfully gotten rid of if you are persistent—repeat, persistent—in treating your pet's ears with medicine, usually a medicated ointment.

Ear mites, if unchecked, can cause deafness in a cat and ultimately kill it. I have seen house cats suffering in pain and total despair with serious cases of ear mites which their owners neglected.

External parasites seem deceptively trivial in an otherwise healthy cat. They don't initially disable the animal. But bear in mind that if you don't mount a fast and effective campaign to rid your animal of them, they can really take over. They can eventually kill your pet, and they present a health hazard to you and your family.

Ringworm

It seems unlikely, doesn't it, but indoor cats are sometimes afflicted with ringworm. They can carry this fungus (it's not a worm at all) a long time before it shows up, so the healthy-looking cat you acquired from a friend, pet shop, or shelter might have it dormant. Then when it finally appears on your cat that hasn't set foot outdoors or had contact with other animals in months, it's hard to believe.

Ringworm appears first as a localized, dime-sized, scaly rash, usually on the tips of the ears, around the nose and eyes. As it enlarges, the animal's hair begins to fall out. You should get prompt veterinary diagnosis and treatment, and be careful about handling your pet because ringworm can be contagious to people—not as much as formerly believed, but still it's best to take precautions. You'll have to give the cat an antibiotic by mouth and bathe it. Throw out the cat's bedding, brushes, collar, and whatever, because there's great danger of reinfection. Clean and vacuum your house, especially the places where the cat lies, and throw the vacuum cleaner bag away.

Keep any cat with ringworm isolated from all other pets—it's contagious to everything except maybe goldfish!

Allergies

Feline allergic reactions can take the form of skin, respiratory, or digestive disorders and, like human allergies, are hard to pinpoint. Also, allergy symptoms are often like those of other illnesses. If a cat has diarrhea and vomiting, is it ill from one of a dozen different diseases—or has it a food allergy? If a cat is sneezing, wheezing, and coughing, does it have a respiratory infection—or is it allergic to something? Are the itchy lesions on a cat's skin caused by a parasite—or an allergy?

Cats have been known to have allergic reactions to foods, flea collars, flea saliva, household products and dyes, tobacco, medicines, and dusty types of kitty litter. Some unfortunate cats are even allergic to catnip!

As with a human allergy, the cure lies in identifying the offending substance. A veterinarian can treat your pet to relieve an allergic reaction—but don't fool around by giving your animal your own antihistamine! If your pet is suspected of having an allergic response to a food, the best course to follow is not to feed the animal at all for two or three days, and then to give it a very bland diet of lamb, chicken, rice, and vegetables, and then gradually add its former foods one at a time until you discover the culprit. (Since most owners find it impossible to fast their pets, who of course beg piteously, some vets recommend hospitalizing for this procedure.)

My cat Olivia once developed a little lesion on her chin that looked like a sore or acne and came and went without healing permanently. It didn't seem to bother her, but there it was on her otherwise perfect face. One morning as she came back to the kitchen after breakfast for her tablespoon of cream, something occurred to me. Unless I picked up the cats' feeding bowls and washed them the minute they finished eating, Dandelion the dog came in and licked them out just in case there were any tasty morsels left. Sometimes I gave Olivia her cream without washing the bowl after Dandelion licked it. I believe the spot on Olivia's chin was caused by an allergic reaction to Dandy's saliva. Sure enough, when I began washing Olivia's bowl *before* pouring in the tablespoon of cream, the spot on her chin healed up and never came back.

Some cats are allergic to plastic feeding bowls. If you notice your cat has a face rash and its nose has lost color, switch to a glass or ceramic bowl.

Diarrhea and constipation

These are tricky symptoms because they can either be indications of serious illness or merely minor, temporary upsets. A healthy cat that is fed a proper diet and carefully groomed is unlikely to become constipated. On the other hand, an older, overweight, or sedentary cat may occasionally suffer from it. Hair balls are a major cause of constipation. A healthy, well-fed cat won't be likely to have diarrhea either—unless it becomes emotionally upset about something. A change in diet can cause either diarrhea or constipation.

If either disorder is the only symptom your cat exhibits, *if* it occurs only temporarily or occasionally, and *if* the animal seems otherwise perfectly healthy, you could try the following home treatments:

For *constipation:*
   Petromalt (follow directions on tube)
   or white petroleum jelly (½ teaspoon), placed behind lower front teeth or rubbed on nose, once a day for two days
   or milk of magnesia, for young cats only (1 teaspoon per ten pounds of body weight), one dose
I don't recommend mineral oil for a cat because if any went down the wrong way while you were administering it, and got in the lungs, the cat could get pneumonia. If any of the above fails to work, take your cat to a veterinarian. Don't neglect it, because the cat could injure itself by constantly straining or could become obstructed.

For *diarrhea:*
   Cooked starchy foods and baby foods
   and Kaopectate (2 teaspoons per ten pounds of body weight) three times a day for two days
   or bone meal mixed in equal amount with baby food
   If diarrhea continues, take your cat to a veterinarian.
   N.B. Don't try home treatments on a kitten with severe diarrhea. It should have immediate medical attention, even with no other symptoms, because it can quickly die from dehydration and weakness.

Hair balls

Most cats, especially older ones and also particularly indoor cats, get hair balls occasionally and vomit them up or expel them. The obvious prevention is simply to brush and brush. You might also give Petromalt several times a week, or put white petroleum jelly (½ teaspoon per ten pounds of body weight) on its nose or behind its front teeth once a week.

Hair balls become a medical problem when they become impacted in the cat's digestive system and cause blockage. The cat will strain unproductively to defecate, or pass small amounts of foul, bloody feces. It may also be lethargic and vomit. See a vet without delay. Blockage may be a surgical emergency.

Heart disease

Because it enjoys a relatively protected life, an indoor cat may live long, and although a cat of any age can have a heart problem, old age is when heart disease is most likely to develop.

Symptoms of heart trouble often develop very suddenly: decreased appetite, subnormal temperature, depression. Within thirty-six hours there will be labored breathing, coughing, swelling of the chest and abdomen, perhaps difficulty in walking. Sometimes the abnormal breathing and coughing may indicate fluid in the lungs.

As you can imagine, heart disease is very serious and needs prompt medical treatment, followed by special care. A cat with a heart problem should not become upset or excited, shouldn't get chilled, and will need a special diet and medication. If the heart problem isn't too serious, the life of a cat that's well taken care of can be prolonged. If the heart disease becomes advanced, the cat may be so uncomfortable, and suffer so much from continually being taken to the vet for treatment, it may be cruel to take heroic measures to extend its life hopelessly.

Between owner and pet

As cat owners know, one of the few comforts of being sick in bed is the constant and seemingly sympathetic company of one's cat. Sympathetic!—mine appear almost glad. "Oh boy, she's gone back to bed!" they seem to say as they pile on after breakfast, to nestle in against me, purring, for the day (and night).

Your cat won't catch whatever it is you've got, not even your runny sniffle.

When your cat is sick, you won't catch its diseases either, with the possible exception of ringworm (see above).

Fleas, of course, are not a feline disease, but you can definitely catch them if your cat or cats are heavily infested.

Your dog can catch fleas from your cat, also ringworm, but otherwise won't get your cat's diseases, and vice versa.

How to administer medicine

The easiest way to give a cat medicine is to put it in its food. This is fine if 1) the cat is eating normally, and 2) the medicine is tasteless, has no noticeable texture, and can be ground fine. Cats are notorious for being able to detect strange taste or texture in their food. One cat owner had success by putting liquid medicine, small amounts at a time, in the sauce from a can of cat food, which her cat lapped. Otherwise, you'll have to get medicine down your cat by force. Unless you're experienced, you might be wise to have somebody help you by holding the cat while you give medicine, or else bundle it so it can't scratch you. Speak soothingly while administering, and praise and stroke the cat afterward. Don't let medicine-giving turn into a confrontation.

Pills: A good vet will prescribe pills in a size suitable for an individual cat, so you won't find yourself trying to get a huge capsule down a small cat.

Quickness counts in giving a pill. Place the cat on a table or counter beside you, facing the same way you are. (If you try to get a pill down a cat while it's facing you, forget it.)

Hug the animal close to your body with your elbow, so your hands are above and behind its head. Open its mouth by pressing the cheeks together behind the upper fangs. Place the pill on the middle of its tongue. (One cat owner coats the pill with butter or mayonnaise, to make it easier to swallow.) Don't throw the pill down the cat's throat, it might go into the windpipe. Close the mouth, hold it shut, and stroke the throat or blow gently on the nose. *Be sure it swallows*. Many owners have let the cat go at this point, certain that the pill was safely on its way to their pet's stomach, only to find it an hour later, surreptitiously spit out in a corner somewhere. When the cat licks its nose, it has swallowed.

Liquids: Unless you have an unusually passive and cooperative cat, an eyedropper works better than a teaspoon. Hold the cat as described above. Don't force the animal's mouth open, but pull out one cheek so a pouch is formed. The cat will be clenching its teeth anyway, so put the dropper in the cheek pouch and squirt the medicine into it. Be careful not to simply squirt or pour the liquid down the back of the cat's throat or you might get it in the windpipe.

Note how much of the stuff your cat spits out, and if it seems to have spattered most of the medicine on you and the surroundings, better try again to be sure you get the prescribed amount down the animal.

Slow motion and patience count in getting a liquid down a cat.

How to take a cat's temperature

You can use a regular rectal thermometer (pediatric size is best). Shake it down to 97° or 98° and cover the tip with plenty of vaseline or petroleum jelly.

It's best if the cat lies on its side or crouches on its belly. Insert the thermometer into the cat's rectum, gently rotating it as it goes in, until it is about half its length. Hold on to your cat firmly while you do this, so it won't take off across the room with the thermometer in. And hold on to the thermometer firmly with your other hand. (Some people have pushed the thermometer in too far and lost it, requiring a veterinarian to get it out.) Your cat will object to all this, but if you do it right, there's no lasting discomfort.

Leave the thermometer in for one full minute. A normal temperature is between 100° and 102.5°, depending on whether the cat is excited, has been racing about, or the weather is very hot. One or two degrees above or *especially below normal* means trouble.

Patient care

It almost goes without saying that you must keep a sick cat warm, out of drafts, and in a quiet spot. Keep its bedding clean. Wipe off any vomit or feces the cat might get on its fur and can't clean off itself—a cat will get terribly upset if it has to lie in its own dirt. Bring its food and water to it, and place a litter box nearby.

N.B. If the sick cat is too weak or depressed to eat, you will have to hand-feed it. (See *Feeding problems*, Chapter Four.) This is very important.

When you first bring your cat home after an operation, feed it only small meals for the first two or three days, and don't let it drink unlimited amounts of water. Since it wasn't fed before and after the surgery, the animal might want to gorge itself on food and water, but this could cause it to vomit. It's better to let it work up to its normal eating habits gradually. Keep an eye on your pet. If it isn't eating, drinking, urinating, and moving its bowels normally within three days after the operation, you should call your veterinarian.

It's important to keep a sick cat's morale up. Otherwise, it can get so depressed it will simply let itself die. Pet it and talk to it encouragingly, give it a lot of support. If it hides, bring it out and pet it. It needs to feel it is important to you. I thought one of my daughter's cats, Linda, was surely done for during an illness, a few years ago. I firmly believe the cat's devotion to my daughter, and hers to it, pulled it through as much as any of the medication and veterinary treatment it received.

If a sick cat must be left alone all day because all the members of the household go to work or school, ask a friend the animal knows to stop in and give it affection during the day. You might also make a tape of your voice talking soothingly and leave it playing for the cat.

One veterinarian I know, who specializes only in cats, employs a nurse whose job it is to take each sick or convalescing cat out of its cage and hold it, pet it, and talk to it—half an hour, twice a day. The vet believes this is an important factor in his patients' recovery.

Unless it needs intensive professional care and life support, a sick cat will do much better at home than in a hospital. An intelligent and caring owner, ministering to the cat under a vet's supervision, can participate dramatically in the cat's recovery.

Neutering

The average unspayed female cat goes into heat (estrus) every twenty-one days from February to September; the unspayed female indoor cat goes into heat every twenty-one days year-round. Unless impregnated immediately, she cries and howls day and night for at least four days, calling for a mate. She'll dart out in a flash every time the door is opened, if you don't grab her. When you go to stroke her, she crouches on her belly with her tail to one side, over her back, and treads with her hind feet. She is clearly uncomfortable. She is also likely to develop serious, medical, "female problems" in later life.

As for the unneutered tom, nobody can tolerate him, poor fellow—especially not indoors—because he smells to high heaven and has a disconcerting habit of spraying urine (highly pungent in odor) all over the house. His need to find a mate is very strong, and like the female in heat, he will figure out ingenious ways to escape the house. Over the years, I have found many intact male cats homeless on the streets, and whether they had escaped from homes or were thrown out because of their smell, nobody knows, but they were certainly down on their luck.

There are many misconceptions about neutering, the most widespread being that it will make the animal fat. The neutered animal may possibly have a somewhat greater tendency to put on weight, in which case you simply adjust the amount of food you give it. But neutering in and of itself will not make a male or female cat fat. Only overeating and lack of exercise will do that.

Other notions about neutering are that it will change the cat's personality, make it lazy, et cetera, et cetera. They're not true either. If anything, neutering might make a cat more sweet and home-loving, but really, that almost totally depends on how you treat it. Neutering will not make it lazy and sluggish.

"Oh, I would never do that to my cat—it's against nature," someone will say. Or, "I wouldn't want to spoil his (or her) fun," says somebody else.

It's hard to argue the "against nature" position, because you could say that birth control by any means by any species is also against nature. What nature is, and what's against nature, are very arbitrary and biased philosophical opinions, seems to me. Is it "natural" for millions of cats to be starving because of unrestrained breeding?

As for the animal's fun, cat owners should guard against

confusing their animals' sexuality with their own. Sex for a cat may be more a matter of relieving an urge than experiencing a profound pleasure. The neutered cat is certainly a lot more comfortable if it doesn't have to endure a constant, powerful urge that's never satisfied.

People who want to let their female cats have litters of kittens "so the children can see the miracle of birth" should follow through and take the kids to an animal shelter to see the caged animals awaiting death—85 percent of the cats and dogs in pounds have to be destroyed because homes cannot be found for them. At this point, there are some 15 million animals in shelters and an estimated 120 million on the streets who will experience the miracle of death, usually with great suffering, because of some people's sentimental and irresponsible attitude about birth.

A *male cat* can be neutered (castrated) at any time after it is six or seven months old. Some veterinarians advise waiting until the animal shows signs of sexual maturity, but since it takes nearly six weeks for the hormone level to decline after castration, you may have to put up with a lot of yowling and spraying if you wait till then. Like any surgery, neutering should be performed when the animal is in good health—don't schedule it when he has a cold or whatever.

The neutering operation for a male is a quite minor procedure. The animal is anesthetized and the testes removed from the scrotal sac through two tiny incisions. Usually you take your unbreakfasted tom to the veterinarian first thing in the morning and pick him up that same evening. He might seem a little groggy, may even refuse dinner, but by the next day he'll be his old self.

Some male cats that are neutered late in life, by the way, continue to mount females and perform—but of course they can't impregnate.

A *female cat* can be neutered (spayed, not "spaded" as some folks erroneously pronounce it) at six or seven months of age. She should not be spayed during a heat cycle because the blood vessels in the uterus are dilated at that time. And of course she should be in good health. Some veterinarians advise waiting until the cat has had her first heat period. There is no truth to the notion that she should have a litter first.

Spaying is a complete ovariohysterectomy—removal of the uterus and ovaries. For this reason, it is a more serious operation than the male's. You will probably be asked not to feed or give your cat water after midnight the night before, and to bring her to the veterinarian first thing in the morning. You can usually pick up your pet the next day. Her belly will have been shaved, and there will be a small incision with a few stitches. Keep her warm and quiet for a few days.

She should go back to the vet about ten to twelve days later to have the stitches removed and for a final checkup to be sure there are no complications (which are rare). If your cat is healthy, and you have a good veterinarian in a decent clinic, a spay operation is perfectly safe.

One side benefit of spaying is that your pet will be far less likely to get breast cancer and will never get the uterine infections so common in older unspayed cats.

There are new drugs that can be given to female cats, by injection or orally, to suppress estrus (the heat cycle), but so far they have not proved safe. Very little is known about the interaction of hormones or the hormone levels of cats. Too many cats have developed mammary tumors, diabetes mellitus, or infections of the uterus from these drugs, and most of the survivors have had to be spayed anyway. Birth-control pills and foods are beginning to be available for people who plan to breed their cats at certain times. But at this point, surgical neutering is still the safest and most beneficial way to prevent estrus and conception in cats.

Since humane shelters and pounds are filled with kittens

who need homes, the back streets and alleys are loaded with homeless cats, and the classified sections of newspapers advertise kittens and cats who need homes, it's a mystery to me why responsible people would allow their cats to bring more into the world. Even if you found homes for the kittens your pet produced, that only means that someone else's kittens would have to be put to death.

The present pet overpopulation problem is so acute that every newborn kitten must be viewed as an indirect public expense. The taxpayer ultimately pays for the kittens that unthinking owners allow their pets to produce. If the kitten goes to a shelter or pound, the public pays for it; if it is adopted into a home, then that home is not available to the next kitten that is brought to the pound or shelter—and so it goes.

I personally believe that there should be a moratorium on all kittening until every homeless cat is adopted. Kitten-mill breeders would of course go out of business, professional breeders would lose some money, and amateur breeders who are not financially motivated would resent curtailing their hobby. But there must be an end to the present situation, which is both immoral and costly. Cats by the millions are starving on the streets, and cats by the millions are being put to death because there are more cats than people can, or will, take care of.

Oh, you will say, but the people who would want a purebred Abyssinian or Birman wouldn't take an ordinary domestic shorthair, and the number of purebred cats is minimal compared to the rest, anyway. But people who have strong preferences for certain purebred cats can often find them in shelters—such animals are available from time to time. A friend of mine recently found a rare, flame-point Siamese kitten in a shelter.

Also, I'm not proposing a permanent end to breeding, just a moratorium of several years until the present crisis in the cat population is brought under control. People who want purebred cats should be prepared to wait a while. Then perhaps there should be permits for very tightly regulated breeding just so the pedigreed breeds won't die out. Many of the best and most responsible breeders (not the kitten-mill type) already try to limit the breeding of show-quality cats. I think that is the direction we should go—in which the reproduction of all cats is regulated, limited by true demand, so none will go homeless, and the pounds will be empty. And instead of the killing, every year, of millions of perfectly healthy cats and kittens, euthanasia can then be used only for cats that are both suffering and incurable.

chapter eight

Behavior Problems and Bad Habits:

How to Avoid or Cure Them

The relationship between the indoor cat and its owner is usually, for better or worse, intense. You can live casually with an indoor-outdoor cat because you aren't thrown together enough to get on each other's nerves—or even to know each other very well. The animal's personality flaws and bad habits are less of a problem (and also its individuality may be less apparent). But when a cat is in your house all the time, not only are you more aware of its beauty, intelligence, and winning ways—you also can't avoid being bothered by any annoying quirks it might develop.

When an indoor cat breaks litter-box training, eats the African violets, or shreds the armchair, most householders quite understandably object. Sometimes a previously well-behaved cat will, apparently out of the blue, acquire a bad habit. Or, you may have adopted an enchanting animal that seems perfect for a few weeks and then settles into a vexing pattern.

There are no sure-fire ways to cure every cat of every bad

habit. But with patience and persistence, you can usually win out—or at least divert the cat to an acceptable alternative. Now and then you can outsmart it. Sometimes punishment works. Occasionally, if you love the cat, you can figure out ways to live with a habit until the animal outgrows it or the cause goes away—or until you discover that you can close your eyes to what it does that bothered you. But understanding some of the classic misbehaviors of cats helps to work out ways to prevent or avoid them.

One caveat—it's important to understand behavior from the cat's point of view. For example, when you leave your cashmere sweater lying on the bed, you might think it is extremely naughty for the cat to make a nest for itself on the sweater, kneading it and pulling threads in the process. But remember that the cat does not regard a sweater the way we do; it has no idea what's wrong with curling up on this nice soft thing it found on the bed. Your cat can never be trained out of doing something as natural as making a nest for itself in a soft spot. It will never learn to recognize a sweater, so how can it be expected to stay off? The only humane and practical thing to do is just not leave anything on a bed, chair, sofa, or whatever that you don't want your cat to lie on. That's not hard to remember. Punishment in such an instance will be confusing and frightening for the animal and make it fearful and withdrawn, even hostile.

The woman, mentioned earlier, who got rid of her first cat because it jumped on the kitchen table did not understand this. You can train a cat not to jump up on some places, but you can't train a cat not to jump up on anything at all, without wrecking its emotional health.

Learn to tell the difference between preventable behavior and innocent, instinctive behavior. Then you won't have unrealistic expectations of your cat.

Breaking litter-box training

One of the most baffling and distressing problems cat owners may be confronted with is to have their previously well-behaved cat start to urinate or defecate in places other than its litter box. It is so out of character for a cat to do this, however, that you can automatically assume it is trying to tell you something: It is sick or upset. This first possibility is the one you should explore instantly, because if the animal is in the first stages of a urinary disorder, you will want to get it to a veterinarian for diagnosis and treatment right away. As explained in Chapter Seven, urinary problems are serious, and if not treated fast, can kill a cat, especially a male, in two days. Inability to hold its urine is one of the symptoms. Excessive urination in and out of the box could mean urolithiasis or perhaps, in older cats, kidney disease or diabetes. So, illness should be ruled out before you explore other reasons for your pet's disconcerting habit.

I suspect that the most common reason for a healthy indoor cat to break training is a dirty box. People who say they wouldn't keep a cat confined in their house or apartment because "cats smell" have usually formed this opinion from visiting other people who are careless about keeping their cats' box clean. Often if a house has an unpleasant cat smell, it may be more than the dirty box that causes it—the cat couldn't stand to go in the dirt and has secretly been relieving itself in a few other places.

Another reason a cat may break training is if the litter box is too small—the cat simply isn't comfortable using it. Or, the box might be in a noisy, public place—a cat trying to use its box in a heavily trafficked spot with children and dogs running through may give up and seek privacy elsewhere. And one cat I know, Linda, likes to have a box to herself rather than share with others. Another cat I heard of stopped using

the box when its owners brought it a nice brand-new box—
the cat preferred its old one.

If your cat is used to one kind of litter, it might not be a
good idea to change suddenly to another type. I remember
putting Becky, who was newspaper trained, into a box with
litter for the first time—she leaped three feet into the air and
hit the floor running.

Sometimes one cat may take to ambushing another when
it's using the box, as I mentioned in connection with the arrival of a second cat, in Chapter Three. In that case, the first
cat may find itself another, secret bathroom, such as the
back of the linen closet. You have to intervene on behalf of
the bothered cat until the two get used to one another.

Often the problem is caused by some kind of environmental stress on the cat—moving to a new house or apartment, the arrival of a new baby, declawing, the marriage of
the owner, workmen in the house, a new pet, or a succession
or accumulation of upsetting changes. Becky broke training
when my daughter went off to college. Cats are creatures of
order and habit and are more susceptible to nuances in the
household than many people realize. Events that may seem
minor to us can be perceived by a pet as catastrophic.

Once you have established that there is nothing physically wrong with your cat, and there's nothing you can do
about an environmental change that might be stressing it
emotionally, then the situation calls for much patience and
for reinstating as much as possible the cat's familiar routine.
And you may even have to start training from the beginning, including confinement, for a while.

Never, never spank or hit a cat. Corporal punishment is
counterproductive with a cat. Even if you succeed in stop-
ping some transgression such as jumping on the kitchen
counter, striking the pet will make it hate and fear you so
much that it will develop other, equally bad and perhaps

more neurotic habits. It definitely will not make a cat use its litter box.

The most you can do in the way of discipline is to shout "No!" when you catch it in the act, and try to pick it up and put it in the litter box. But the cat will not just stand there and wait for you when you shout and begin to run toward it —it will take off. By the time you have chased and captured it, it will be frightened and will have forgotten what it did anyway, and you'll have a trail of urine to clean up.

Some people recommend punishing the cat by making it sniff something acrid such as vinegar at the spot where it has soiled. You put the vinegar or other pungent-smelling stuff on a rag, carry the cat to the spot, and make it smell the rag. I have no idea if this works, but you might give it a try.

Other people recommend throwing a magazine at the animal or squirting it with a water pistol or plant sprayer when you see it beginning to relieve itself someplace other than in its box. Seems to me these are good ways to make a cat think that if it has to perform these natural functions, it will be hit with a flying object or with water. Then not only will you be in an adversary position with your pet, but you'll have a real neurotic on your hands. Also, the cat may learn to urinate only when you're not looking.

It *is* a good idea to scrub each place where it has soiled with a strong detergent or cleaner to get rid of the odor of the cat's urine, so it won't be attracted to return to that place (cats tend to go back to spots they have soiled). Don't use ammonia or any ammonia-based product for this purpose, however, because ammonia is a component of urine and will simply act to lure the cat back to the spot. Some cat owners have had good results by putting some mothballs in the spot after cleaning it. Mothballs, by the way, can also be sprinkled in a flowerpot if your cat has chosen the potting soil around your house plants as its bathroom. But remember mothballs are toxic if the cat should get them on its paws and then lick them, so cover or enclose the mothballs in cheesecloth or some such.

When my daughter had a loft apartment, she had quite a few large potted plants on the floor. One of her cats couldn't resist urinating in the soil. My daughter solved that problem by taping strips of masking tape across the top of the pots in a grill pattern, with spaces between the strips for the plants and for watering, but no access to the soil itself for the cat. Chicken wire can also be fitted over a pot, with a hole in the middle for the plant; that's less noticeable than masking tape.

If a cat has soiled on a bed or sofa, cover it with a sheet of plastic until you have retrained the animal. The cat is not likely to want to urinate on a slick surface where it's sure to get its feet wet.

If you have to retrain your pet, confine it when you're not at home. A small room such as a bathroom is best. (As a precaution against returning to chaos, however, you better remove the towels and toilet paper. The cat will pull the towels onto the floor and festoon the room with toilet paper.) Don't shut the cat in a room where it has previously misbehaved. Or, you might get a safari cage at a pet supply store and confine it in that. These large folding mesh cages can be set up anywhere in the house where the animal will be comfortable. Leave it food, water, a bed—and a clean litter box.

When you're at home, let the cat have the run of the house. It will probably have used the box while confined, so freedom from the bathroom or safari cage can be its reward. Put several boxes around the house, and keep an eye on the cat. It will usually signal when it's about to relieve itself; it searches around, maybe mews, and when it begins to scratch and turn in circles in one spot, that's probably the moment. Pick it up and place it in a litter box. You might also encourage it with what works for a young kitten—put a paper towel moistened with the animal's own urine or feces in the litter box as a lure. Then when the cat performs in the box, pet it and praise it.

Keep in mind that once your cat does begin to use the box again, you can then reinforce the good behavior with rewards and praise. Cats can usually be trained with Skinnerian technique, rarely by punishment.

Scratching furniture

Before discussing this very real problem, I suggest you please read *Your cat's nails* in Chapter Five, so for starters you'll know your cat is not trying to destroy your furniture or bug you, but is quite innocently performing a natural self-grooming rite. Some cats seem to need to do this more than others. Some will shred your upholstery in a matter of weeks; others scratch so minimally that you hardly notice where they have done it.

The best way to deal with a cat's urge to dig its claws into the furniture is to provide it with a good scratching post. There are all kinds of posts on the market. The most common one is an upended log on a small wooden base—but I have never known a cat that would actually use this type. For one thing, they tip easily, and no cat is going to work out on anything unsteady.

One very successful device I've seen is a cork cylinder affixed to a plaque that you attach upright on your wall at a height comfortable for the cat to reach standing on its hind legs. But these cork things seem to be hard to find in stores.

Far and away the best type of pole is upholstered in heavy carpeting and fixed securely to a broad, heavy, upholstered base, or a similarly upholstered tension pole secured between the floor and ceiling. You can make one of these yourself, or buy one. Some are simple with just the base and

pole and maybe a little carpeted platform on top big enough
for one cat to sit on. Others are elaborate with several sitting
platforms and even little houses that the animals can nap in.
It's important that the pole be tall enough—it should accommodate a cat standing on its hind legs.

Menelaus, a cat I mentioned earlier, wasn't interested in
an upholstered post until his owner covered it in denim. She
had noticed that he liked to scratch at her legs when she
was wearing jeans, so she cut off a pair of jeans and made
shorts out of them, took the leftover denim and sewed it
onto the scratching post. Menelaus got the point right away
and has been using the post ever since.

Some cats like an upholstered hollow cube that they can
use both as a scratching place and a snug bed.

It's easy to train a kitten to use one. Every time you see
the kitten starting to work on a rug or chair, pick it up and
hold it with its paws in a good scratching position on the
pole, then move its paws gently and suggestively back and
forth. Praise it extravagantly while you do this. After a few
times, the kitten will get the idea.

Some adult cats take to these good scratching posts right
away and never go back to the arm of the sofa. Some cats,
alas, will have nothing to do with them. My Olivia adores
ours, works out on it several times a day, and never uses the
furniture, but Fred and Gina just go limp and act annoyed
when I try to show them how to use it. It's true I acquired it
after they were middle-aged and set in their ways, but then,
Olivia was five years old, no kitten. I praise her so much
while she's scratching away on it, she does it assiduously
about ten times a day, sometimes looking over her shoulder
at me to be sure I notice.

When Gina was a kitten, she used to climb up the leg of
anyone who was wearing pants. Maybe if I had got her a
denim-covered scratching post, she'd be using that instead
of my rugs.

If I catch Fred or Gina scratching the furniture or rugs, I yell "No!" and they'll look at me and stop doing it—for the moment. I also pick them up and carry them to the post and try to encourage them to use it. Maybe Olivia has given Fred and Gina the notion that the post is *hers*. (Someone has suggested that they may simply be disgusted with her for currying my favor in such an obvious way.) I plan to make room for another and try to persuade Fred and Gina that it's *theirs*. I haven't given up yet. Meanwhile, I trim their nails regularly so they're not so destructive (see Chapter Five).

I've heard of people keeping a water pistol or plant sprayer handy and squirting their cat every time it starts in on the furniture or rug. An empty aerosol can would do as well, because a cat won't like the hiss or the stream of air. One cat owner I know keeps a spray can of air (the kind used for dusting) on the sofa when she's out. The cat has learned to dislike having air squirted on it, and just the sight of the hateful can keeps it away.

Catnip rubbed into the carpeting of a scratching pole also acts to attract cats to it. A toy attached to the top would lure a kitten or young cat, but don't use a rubber band for this because if the cat pulled the toy off and ate any of the rubber band, it could get seriously sick (see Chapter Six).

If you have a large house or apartment, several posts are better than just one. I also think it's a good idea to keep a platform pole in front of a window; a cat will like to sit on the platform and look out the window, and this will encourage it to use the pole for scratching too.

There are cat-repellent sprays on the market that claim to protect furniture and rugs by infusing them with a harmless scent that cats don't like. I have never heard of one that worked. Either cats don't mind the scent, or the scent doesn't linger on the furniture or rugs long enough to repel the cats.

Declawing

Now, as to the matter of declawing (surgical removal of the claws of the front paws). This is a hotly controversial subject. To some people, the operation is a mutilation from which the pet never fully recovers emotionally; other folks claim it doesn't hurt the cat a bit and it never misses its claws. The anti-declawing faction points out, correctly, that you can never allow a declawed cat outdoors even for a minute for the rest of its life, because if it were threatened by dogs or cruel children, it might not be able to defend itself or climb a tree to safety. The pro-declawers say that a lot of people who would not put up with an animal that damaged the upholstery will take a declawed cat and give it a good home, so declawing gets cats into homes, which may be true but begs the question.

I myself have known declawed cats who apparently have not been harmed, physically or emotionally, one bit. I have also heard horror stories from veterinarians who have seen cats suffer and die from declawing surgery. And I have known some cats who became highly timid or aggressive after their claws were removed.

Some veterinarians and breeders say that declawing a very young nursing kitten, five to fifteen days old, hardly bothers it at all. Others say you can safely declaw a grown cat but *never* a kitten. A few veterinarians refuse to declaw cats of any age. And most of the cat care books by veterinarians that I have read do not oppose declawing, but seem reluctant about it. They say, "Declaw if all else has failed," or "only as a last resort."

A cat owner contemplating having his or her pet declawed should be aware that it is not a simple operation, and there can be serious postoperative complications that are not uncommon:

1) The paws can hemorrhage two or three days later. If the hemorrhage is not checked immediately, the cat can bleed to death.

2) If the bandages are too tight, gangrene can set in, and as a result the paws have to be amputated.

3) If the declawing is done poorly and bone chips are left in, the paws will periodically become infected. Then the operation must be done over.

My impression is that the books that are sanguine about declawing do not explain these dangers.

Some declawed cats definitely undergo a personality change—they become nervous and defensive. They seem to try to make up for their lack of claws by becoming hostile, especially outside their own home environment, such as at the veterinarian's or in a strange house.

I have deep reservations about declawing. Let's put it this way: I would never have it done to my own cats. And I don't recommend it for yours.

Eating house plants

Again, there seems to be a wide variation among cats, in terms of predilection for house-plant eating. Some cats will chew on the leaves of anything green and growing; others won't; and some will decimate certain plants but not others.

One possible explanation might be the animal's food—it has been suggested that a cat that gets a well-balanced and varied diet including vegetables will be less likely to eat plants. But there seem to be some properly fed cats that like to nibble on plants just for the hell of it. I think this is particularly true of single cats—they are more likely to get into plants when their owners are away, simply to relieve their boredom and loneliness. Or, some cats will chew plants when they're angry at their owners. When Pushkin is displeased about something, he'll hang around a plant till he's sure his owner is looking, and then deliberately take a bite.

However, it's also possible that a pair of kittens who have each other to play with might, even so, join forces to work over a plant out of pure mischief. So sometimes a cat will not necessarily eat a plant but damage it by playing with it. Spider plants, for instance—what cat in its right mind could resist those dangling fronds? When my spider plant outgrew its hanging pot, I had to give it to a catless friend. Ferns and palms also seem to attract playful cats. You can always hang your ferns out of reach; palms are more of a problem. Mothballs around the base might be a deterrent (but be sure to cover or enclose them in something so the cat can't nibble them or get them on its paws, since they're toxic).

Another way to protect your plants from your cats is to cage them—the plants, not the cats. Pretty greenery in old-fashioned birdcages can be very decorative.

Another deterrent that might work on a hardy plant is painting the leaves with Tabasco or other hot food sauce. The cat might hate the taste enough to stop after one bite. Spraying the plants with a solution of white vinegar and water might work also—especially if you put a drop of vinegar full strength on the cat's tongue at the same time. The taste of the plant will then remind the cat of that bitter taste on its tongue. (Be sure not to spray the vinegar-water solution on the cat; it will hurt its eyes.)

Some cat experts recommend growing a pot of catnip or wheat grass just for the cat. I personally wonder if this might confuse the animal. If it's okay to chew one plant, the animal figures, why not the others? But I suppose if you put the cat's plant totally separate from yours, and worked hard at reprimanding it when it went near your plants but praised and petted it when it ate its own, this might be successful.

And as I pointed out in Chapter Six, certain plants could be a health hazard to a persistent nibbler. If your cat is one of those, it's best to stick to the safe plants and not have the poisonous ones in your home at all unless you can hang them well out of your cat's reach.

Nursing

This is an exotic problem but common enough to deserve mention. It usually starts when the cat is a kitten and is considered rather touching and sweet—the cat sucks on its owner's finger, arm, or throat, or sometimes on clothing, as if it were nursing. The cat closes its eyes, kneads with its paws, and purrs contentedly. Some owners don't mind this, while others do. And some cats nurse a lot, some only occasionally, and others never.

I heard of one kitten that nursed at its owner's beard. And Pushkin used to nurse at his owner's sleeve until it would be wringing wet. It's not unusual for a cat to drool while nursing.

Nobody knows why some cats do this. One theory is that they were orphaned or weaned too early and never got the nursing instinct out of their systems. However, it's not a symptom of physical ill health.

Endearing as this habit may be in a little kitten, it's just plain annoying when your fifteen-pound cat wakes you several times a night nursing at the sleeve of your pajama or your neck. Most kittens outgrow it, but if your cat is still doing it by the time it reaches adolescence, you should discourage it. Just push the animal away when it starts in. If it persists, say "No!" and blow on its nose or tap its nose with your finger. Be firm. Don't put up with it one time, then get mad the next.

Some cats nurse on themselves—on their tail or leg, even keeping it up until they've rubbed off the hair and made the skin raw. Kittens have been known to nurse on one another and can actually do harm. I have never had a cat that nursed, but I suspect the phenomenon may be related to boredom and stress. Zoo animals confined alone in cramped, bare cages and deprived of activity and stimulation are known to actually mutilate themselves. I suggest that when an indoor cat does this, it is suffering from the same kind of stress. If you get the animal a companion, and do whatever you can to make its environment more interesting—give it toys, play with it, provide it the opportunity to look out a window where there are birds, people, action to watch—it should stop.

Crying

A healthy cat that cries when its owners are out is bound to be lonesome, and the only good solution for this is to get it a friend. If for some reason you really are limited to a single cat, and can't even have a dog, parakeet, or hamster so it isn't the only living creature at home for hours on end when you're away, then you might try consoling it in other ways.

Some owners have found that keeping a radio playing softly helps.

Others have even made tape recordings of their own voices and left these playing. Also, a good window perch where the animal can while away the time watching the outside world gives it something to do—it's like TV for us.

Another ploy you might try is to play hard with your pet for as long as possible in the morning before you leave the house. If you tire it out, it might sleep most of the day.

If a cat you've had for some time suddenly begins to cry even when you're home, then of course you want to find out if there's something physically hurting it. It might be sick, or it might have a problem like that poor cat's I mentioned at the end of Chapter Five, that had a wad of fur painfully stuck under its tooth.

I've heard of some indoor cats that wake the household by

crying in the middle of the night or especially at early hours. They are not necessarily lonely single cats, and they're not hungry. Nobody knows why they do it. I'm not talking about the well-regulated cat who hasn't adjusted to a time change and wants his breakfast at five o'clock when all the clocks say six. I mean the chronic early-morning riser who wanders about the house making mournful sounds waking everybody up.

One theory has been advanced that such a cat is bored, there's not enough stimulation in its life, and it feels it more poignantly when everything is quiet. Perhaps a dog would be a good companion for it; a dog, being a diurnal animal, might play with the cat enough during the day to tire it out.

I wonder if a cage of hamsters or mice would distract the cat. Cats have been known to watch these creatures in utter fascination for hours. Another idea might be an aquarium—just as interesting to a cat, and quieter. Also, owners of early-morning criers might try leaving the shades or curtains up at one interesting window so the cat can sit and watch early-morning activity outdoors. A tree full of birds, or a street with early-bird people passing, might keep a cat quiet for an hour or so.

Aggressiveness

A cat that has a bad habit of ambushing people's ankles, biting, or scratching has usually been abused at some time in its past and never been properly socialized. Or, it may simply have been played with roughly as a kitten. A cat with aggressive habits left over from kittenhood, when pouncing or biting was regarded as cute, just has a crude sense of humor (see Chapter Nine). This type of aggressiveness is not the same as that of a cat that is antisocial from fear.

The animal that has been tormented by human beings requires a lot of patience, but it is a very creative and rewarding experience to gain its trust. We once took in a huge black male cat (Eldridge, mentioned earlier) that had been through the mill. His front legs were splayed in such a way that they looked as if they had once been broken and healed without being set. He had a thin line of a scar under the fur around his throat that suggested he'd been tortured in a way that I don't even want to think about. Some of his teeth were broken off. And when we found him, he was unneutered, sick, and vicious. I'd never had a cat in such bad shape. He was a challenge.

Somehow I got him to a veterinarian who treated him for urinary disorder. We kept him quiet in a bathroom for a few days until he was well, and then had him neutered. Little by little, with lots of good care and reassurance, he came around. In fact, Eldridge became a jolly and gentle cat, a friend to all the human beings, cats, and dogs in the household.

On the other hand, there was Cleopatra—heaven knows what her early experiences on the street had been, but she never completely recovered from them emotionally. She growled and shrank from everybody but her owner, bit and scratched if you persisted in handling her—all her life.

There is no sure cure for every aggressive cat that has had traumatic early experiences with human beings or other cats. All I can say is that in most instances, lots of love and good care will make a real pussycat out of a hellcat that is savage from early abuse.

If you have had a normally loving relationship with your indoor cat and it suddenly, or even gradually, becomes aggressive, you want to first find out if it is in some kind of physical or emotional pain. A small but deep wound, a bad tooth, chronic ear infection, or arthritis are just a few of the disorders that can cause a cat to become cranky. And in rare instances, cats do develop brain tumors that turn them into ferocious and dangerous animals.

The same emotional stress that might make a previously well-behaved cat break litter-box training can ruin its disposition. Or, confinement in too close quarters—keeping it in one room all the time, say—could certainly be a cause. Sexual frustration in an unneutered cat might make it aggressive.

Aggressiveness should not be confused with a cat's startle reaction. Every owner has had the experience of being scratched by his or her own docile and affectionate cat when it was startled or frightened. Be careful picking up your cat when the vacuum cleaner is running, there's a new cat or dog around, or anything else is happening that might trigger the animal's always-ready fight-or-flight response. To this day I have a scar on my arm from having Fred (of all cats!) in my arms when someone standing close to me turned on an electric drill.

The natural human reaction, when a cat bites or scratches you, is to smack it. Sometimes the bite or scratch is so startling and painful you can't help it. My feeling is that we should try to control the impulse; I have never yet known or even heard of a cat that was cured of any bad habit by being hit, without a concomitant bad effect on its personality. I have known cats that became neurotic and fearful, even vicious, from being struck every time they misbehaved. Corporal punishment, even in cases of aggressiveness, just won't work. You have to achieve your goal by other means.

By the way, another human reaction when a cat grasps your hand, biting and scratching, is to pull away. Try not to do it, you'll only get hurt worse. Grit your teeth and pry the animal away gently, saying "No!" quietly but firmly.

Love bites, incidentally, should not be mistaken for hostility. Some cats show affection and pleasure by gently nibbling the finger of someone who's petting them. Fred sometimes does this when he gets carried away.

When a cat behaves aggressively toward other cats, it

might be a symptom of illness. I'm not talking about the normal caterwauling and fur-flying that goes on when strange cats first meet; I mean the rare cases where a physically healthy cat is truly dangerously aggressive toward other cats. The poor animal is probably mentally ill. If a cat grew up on the street where it had to battle other cats for every mouthful of food to stay alive, it may be permanently imprinted with those experiences. You can't inflict such an animal on a normal indoor cat or cats. You have to find it a home where it will be the only cat or, if that's not possible, euthanize it.

Sometimes aggression among cats is caused by some shift in the pecking order, a challenge to the dominant cat. A friend describes the way her cat Charles handled a young, upwardly mobile male cat that periodically defied him. Charles was heavy and knew it. When he'd had enough, he would seize the challenger by the scruff of the neck, throw him down, and then simply sit on him. He'd look up blandly as if he had no idea there was another cat flattened out under him. Eventually Charles would stand up and walk away, leaving the chastened young male to get up off the floor and pull himself into shape again. Cats have to work out pecking-order problems themselves.

Scolding a cat

Asserting your authority without hitting can definitely instill guilt in a cat and possibly control behavior to a limited extent. In my house, for example, the cats aren't allowed on the kitchen counter next to the sink where I prepare food. I can make Fred, say, get down simply by yelling at him, even from the next room. But it would be a mistake to think the fear of my anger would seriously deter him from getting up there if fish or something else good were on the counter and I weren't around.

One cat owner scolds his cat in a deep voice, which seems to impress the cat enough to make it feel guilty. A stern command from him will make the cat stop doing something naughty—raiding the garbage, for instance. But it's unlikely that the fear of a scolding alone would keep a cat with healthy appetite and curiosity out of the garbage permanently. In other words, scolding will deter at a given moment, but fear of scolding will rarely prevent. You really have to outsmart the animal or retrain it into good behavior that is as agreeable to it as the bad behavior.

I know one cat that is thrilled to pieces when her brother gets scolded. Mary Jane is a sweet, passive cat that is quite overshadowed by smart, assertive, extroverted Ivan. But when Ivan gets into trouble and is rebuked by their owners, Mary Jane comes running to watch in delight. Then she becomes very frisky and full of herself, cavorting about the house showing off. Mary Jane is a different cat for however long Ivan is in the doghouse. Even though she seems to love her brother, she obviously has some jealous feelings too.

The cat burglar.

Many cats are as good at fetching as dogs are, and it can be a favorite game.

Curiosity, combined with intelligence, helps a cat find a way to investigate many places.

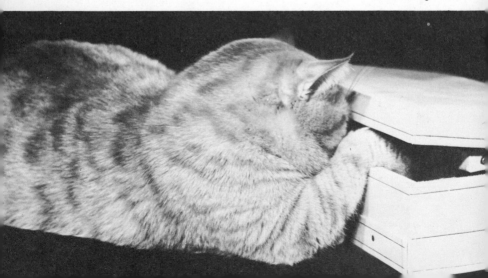

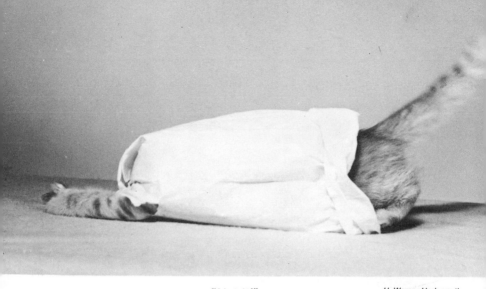

"Got it!"

This playful cat likes to sit on the canopy of a four-poster and tap people on the head as they walk by.

Dripping water may provide hours of entertainment. This cat is trying to see where the drops are coming from.

A porcelain washbowl has just the right contours and feels nice and cool on a hot day.

A cat who couldn't make up its mind whether to lie on the chair or the table has apparently fallen asleep trying to decide.

You might say there are two works of art on this table.

The ability of a cat to loll gracefully even on hard surfaces is one of the animal's great decorative assets.

Favorite sitting places: in baskets, bags, and boxes.

A kitten can engender beautiful feelings of tenderness in a child.

Mary Bloom

John Gajda, Detroit, MI

This kitten might be saying, "I've always wanted my very own dog!"

Cats often have surprising friends.

Hope Ryden

chapter nine

Communication and Play:
Keeping Your Cat Happy
and Loving

There once lived in New York City a physician who shared a
large terraced apartment with his two cats. He was a very
distinguished, somewhat dignified doctor, and he really
liked his cats. One Saturday morning he received a phone
call from the superintendent of his building saying that if he
saw a man walking around on his terrace, he shouldn't be
alarmed because that would be the roofer inspecting the
condition of all the terraces.

The doctor put on his bathrobe and looked out on his terrace. It was a fine spring morning. Then one of his pets
twined around his ankles and ran suggestively toward the
kitchen, indicating that it was time for breakfast. The doctor
left the terrace door open and went to feed his cats. They
paced the kitchen floor impatiently. Their owner filled their
feeding bowls and bent down to watch them with satisfaction as they ate.

"How're my sweetums?" he crooned fondly. "Did ums
wantum breakfoo? Well, Daddy gave his little dumplings
nice breakfoo."

"Ahem," boomed a voice in back of him. Startled, the physician turned to see a very big man in work clothes looking at him disgustedly. "You the doc?" the fellow growled with obvious scorn.

Seems to me that's the kind of episode most cat lovers can relate to.

Conversing with your cat

It's hard not to baby-talk to your cat—cats are so responsive. They love endearing tones, chuckles, whispers, singsong, falsetto—the whole bit. They also enjoy it when you imitate *their* sounds.

"Meow," says Olivia as she helps me make my bed in the morning.

"Meow," I reply, sounding just like her. "Meow, meow, meow," she continues, and I answer in kind, and so it goes. Sometimes I wonder precisely what we are saying to each other, but it's an affectionate dialogue, certainly.

Some of my cats' repertory of sounds are easy to imitate, and when I'm doing it, I defy most people to tell our voices apart. Other sounds, such as the trill, I can't make with my particular human vocal equipment—nor can I give a convincing purr. But it's fun to try, and the cats seem to get a kick out of it.

People who know cats learn to recognize not only their own pets' voices and the different meanings of their sounds but the utterances that are common to all cats. Just as you can tell by listening to a perfect stranger whether an outburst such as "Oh!" means he or she is enjoying a joke, greeting a friend, surprised, exultant, in deep trouble, or simply trying to get someone's attention, you can tell all this and more from listening to cats.

Depending on its tone, a cat's meow, trill, murmur, cry, howl, or other sound can mean:

Hello.
You've been gone too long! I've missed you!
I need my dinner. He (she) forgot to feed me!
Hurry up with breakfast.
I feel playful—how about a game?
I'm pretending to be a ferocious tiger chasing my prey!
Ow—that's my tail you're stepping on!
What are you doing?
What have you got in that bag?
I'm terrified. Please don't take me to the vet!
I hate the new cat!
I hear another cat outside.
Oh boy, look at that bird out there in the tree!
Oh, it's you here on the sofa—how cozy. Let's cuddle.
Look what an adorable pussycat I am. You should pet me.
I'm cold out here on the porch—let me in!
I'm lost!!!
I'm in desperate need of a home. Please! Take me in!
I'm starving. Have you got anything to eat?
I love you.
Look at this fine mouse I've brought you.
and a whole range of other messages.

I firmly believe that most of the factors that determine whether an individual cat is dull or interesting are in direct proportion to the amount and quality of attention shown the animal by the owner. A cat who is just *there*, ignored except for being fed and given routine care, will keep to itself and will appear to be a boring pet. It cohabits with its owners, sometimes amicably enough, but there is no real rapport, no deep mutual affection and concern, and some of the most engaging aspects of cat personality will wither from lack of development and nurturing.

Talking to your cat, whether you look into its face and speak to it in your normal voice, or kitchy koo over it, or reply to it in the same sounds it makes, will not only make your bond with your pet closer, but will make it a more communicative and responsive animal.

Cat body language

People who don't know cats may accuse you of being anthropomorphic when you talk about cats' expressions. But when you know cats, you realize how expressive they can be without opening their mouths.

The muscles of a cat's face are limited, compared to ours. The animal can sneer and do a few little things with its mouth. But the eyes! What a variety of expressions a cat can make by changing the shape of its eyes.

Cats can give you a round-eyed stare, they can narrow their eyes to slits and blink slowly with pleasure, they even have a way of flattening the upper lids in a straight horizontal line when they are insulted or perplexed. They can open their eyes wide in anxiety when they're imploring you to do something for them (feed, open the door, hand something down). But that look is different from the wide-eyed innocent, "Who, me?"—you see that one, of course, when you find the garbage tipped over or the flowers pulled out of a vase and chewed. If Gina could speak when she gives me that look, she'd have me believe that Dandelion got up on my desk and rolled all the pencils off. Menelaus' owner claims he can even furrow his brow in a worried way and pull in his cheeks to make his face look thin and hollow when he puts on his starving-cat act. I believe it.

Cats can also use the pupils of their eyes. Anger, even make-believe fury when they're playing, can widen the pupils so the eyes appear almost black. Whether or not this eye action is conscious, as our smiles can be, is immaterial, really. Whether the animal deliberately uses the eyes to express itself, or the eyes simply follow the emotions it feels, they are nevertheless good clues to its thoughts and feelings.

The ears work in harmony with the eyes. There's the alert, ears-forward position; the semialert, ears-up-but-pointed-sideways position; and of course the flattened-back position that goes with fear or anger (real or pretend). But there's also a flattened-down-sideways position, which the ears may assume when the cat feels ambivalent or puzzled, and also when you're scratching the top of its head.

In addition to the eyes and ears, the cat's whole body communicates. There's the compact crouch with the fur fluffed up, which the cat assumes when it's cold, or the curled-in-a-ball, tail over the eyes, when it's snugly asleep in a cold room. Then there's the summer sprawl: flat on the back, legs extended, exposing as much of the body as possible to the air currents. There's the playing crouch, the observing crouch, the patiently waiting crouch. There's the indignant stalk, the saunter, the trot, the romp, the gallop, the sneak, the cautious walk, the frightened speed-of-light streak.

Cats, who are capable of walking so silently they almost slither, can also stomp. They stiffen their legs and come down hard with their body weight. They may do this on you when they want your attention. Sometimes Olivia does this to wake me up. She'll start with her paw-pat—a gentle little press on my face or neck with her paw, claws in, just the pad of the paw. After a while, if paw-pats haven't roused me, she'll resort to the stomp. This consists of sudden gallops across my sleeping body, stiff-legged jumps that can only be described as stomps. In her case, they work. I am hardly disturbed at all by paw-pats. Stomps really get a body up.

Some people have said that the face rub, which a cat usually does against its owner's hand when being petted, is to release a scent from little glands on the face of the cat. I have no idea if this is true; I only know all cats do it in response to a caress.

A cat approaching to be petted arches its back and carries its tail straight up. Gina also curls her front paws one after the other as she walks, then makes a 180-degree turn when she reaches you, throws herself down and rolls on her back with the front paws dangling under her chin and her "Aren't I adorable?" look on her face. Olivia doesn't go in for that coquettish stuff—hers is the direct approach. When she decides she likes you, she jumps into your lap and presents her rear, tail up, then lies full length on your thighs with her front paws over your knees. Fred walks up stiffly and with deliberate dignity sits down beside you on the sofa.

When you see a cat approach a strange cat with hostility, real or pretend, you may notice it bending its head down sideways in a funny way. That's because a cat's best fighting position is on its back, so a frightened or aggressive cat (or a play-fighting one) may instinctively be preparing to roll onto its back and gets its head into position for the roll, just in case.

The owners of indoor cats are in a better position to notice the whole range of cats' body language because whatever the cat does, it's right there for you to see. Also, the communication between a caring cat owner and the pet is greatly developed. The cat really "talks" to you because you are so important to it.

Games cats play

Remember that the domestic cat's wild cousins—lions, bobcats, pumas, and the like—spend from sixteen to twenty hours a day sleeping or lying quietly, and there's no reason to believe your pet's species is different. So you don't have to feel guilty if your indoor cat lies around sleeping or dozing most of the time. You're not depriving it of a life that would normally be highly active.

Nevertheless, I think owners of indoor cats should spend some time every day playing with their animal, just to help keep it alert, content, and slender. And this will enhance your pleasure in having the cat in the first place.

Next to sleeping and eating, playing seems to be an essential activity for a cat. Even indoor cats are not totally dependent on their owners for entertainment. One of their greatest assets is that they don't just sit there waiting for you to provide them with something to do—they find ingenious ways of amusing themselves.

Our cat Becky used to like to sit in the window whenever it was snowing outside and try to catch the snowflakes that fell against the windowpane. Gina likes to delicately knock a pen or pencil off my desk and roll it around the floor. My daughter's cat Phoebe will tip over the wastebasket by her drawing table and explore the contents. My son's cat Baxter used to work out on the railing of the stairwell—he'd curl himself around it till he could grab his tail with his front paws between his hind feet and exercise himself that way.

Indoor cats will play with the leaves of a plant, stare at a tankful of fish or a cage of hamsters, play-fight with the fringe of a rug, roll a toy around. They love to sit and look out of windows, watching everything that is going on in the street, yard, or building next door. Best of all, they like to play with each other or with you.

One caution, however: Be careful how you play with a cat, especially a kitten. Some people waggle their hand in front of a cat to encourage it to box. It may be amusing when a little eight-week-old kitten bats at your hand or grabs it and rolls on its back, biting your fingers and kicking with its tiny hind feet. But when that same kitten grows up to be a seventeen-pound cat and does the very same thing, it is not cute at all—it hurts. A lot. A kitten ambushing your

wiggling fingers is harmless; a grown cat doing it is painful—
but it's all the same to the cat. The cat, of course, can't understand why it gets scolded or smacked for trying to play a
game that you encouraged in the first place.

A good rule to follow faithfully is *never play with a cat
with your hands, fingers, or toes.* A cat should never be encouraged to play by biting, swatting, scratching, grabbing,
or otherwise fastening on to any part of your anatomy.
You'd be surprised how many people do this, particularly
with a kitten.

There's a theory that zoo animals need some form of stalking, chasing, and being chased to keep their natural hunting
instincts from atrophying. While domestic cats have been
kept by human beings for a couple of thousand years, cats
still seem to have a vestigial urge to stalk, chase, and capture. Many games you can play with your cat are of this nature.

Pounce: When you drag the sash of your bathrobe across
the floor and your pet dashes after it and pounces on it, it's
not hard to guess what the cat is pretending. A piece of
heavy paper tied to the end of a string is great to swing in
the air over a cat's head or up and down against a doorframe. Even sixteen-year-old Fred will stand on his hind
legs and try to catch a string dangled against a doorframe.

A good version of Pounce is played by the owner sitting
cross-legged on the floor. (This one from Menelaus' owner.)
You trail a knotted string around your body, or under one
knee. The cat will chase it around you, over and under your
knees. You can also do this one sitting in an upholstered
chair with the string dangled over the back or over one arm.

Some people, by the way, have found that their cat will
play with the beam of a flashlight. An elderly or bedridden
person might have fun this way with a cat in a darkened
room.

Another form of Pounce can be played in bed (and this is the only instance in which your fingers or toes should be used as bait). Wiggle them under a good thick covering of bedclothes, or move them back and forth, scratching the sheets with your fingernails. The cat will go into a paroxysm of biting and pummeling and have great fun at this without hurting you. And I have found that this rough play, by the way, will not make the animal continue to do this when your hands and toes are exposed. Cats aren't that dumb—they understand that under the blankets is another matter.

Hide-and-seek: When you're playing with your cat, try this: Peek around a door at your cat and then draw back quickly. Peek again. Most cats love this, will try to sneak up on you, or will retreat and then peek out at you. Menelaus, for example, will keep this up till he thinks his owners don't know he's there. Then he'll sneak up and try to surprise them. Sometimes they leap out at him, and he'll dash back behind his door and start over. Other times they let him think he's surprised and scared them, which he seems to think is great fun.

Fred likes to play a version of this when I'm in the bathtub. He sneaks up and sits on the mat, and I'll sink down till I'm lying in the water where he can't see me. All is quiet. Suddenly he'll pop up with his front paws on the edge of the tub and peek in at me as if to say "Boo!", his eyes huge and black. Then I sit up, splashing the water, and he runs away in great confusion. Fifteen seconds later he's back.

Retrieve: You might test your cat to see if it is a retriever. Some cats are born retrievers, some not. I don't know how to teach a nonretriever to retrieve. But try throwing a toy, something easily portable such as a ball of paper, and see if your pet picks it up and starts back toward you. If it does, take the cue and throw the object again. The cat might get the idea and bring it back to you, or you might have to try it during several play sessions before the cat catches on.

Baxter used to love this game more than anything in the world and would keep it up for as long as anyone would play with him. He would bring the wad of paper right to your feet and stand there looking up at you eagerly, waiting for you to throw it again for him. He especially loved it when you threw the wad of paper down the stairs—he'd dash down four or five steps at a time (thud, thud, thud) and quickly come scampering back up with the paper in his mouth. This provides wonderful exercise for an indoor cat if you can get yours to do it.

Capture: My son plays this with his athletic yellow cat Fidel. He holds a twisted pipe cleaner (Fidel's favorite toy) at arm's length about six or seven feet above Fidel's head. The cat will sit perfectly still and look up at it for some seconds. Then suddenly he'll shoot straight up into the air and capture the pipe cleaner with his front paws—usually to the applause of anyone watching, because the leap itself is truly stunning.

Fidel will keep this up repeatedly until he's finally exhausted, then he'll flop down on his side and rest awhile till he's ready for more.

Carry: This isn't really a game but just something many cats enjoy: being carried about. Menelaus likes to be held over his owner's shoulder and walked around and allowed to investigate places he can't otherwise reach. Olivia, believe it or not, likes to be danced. One evening there was some especially lively music on the radio, and as I was walking through the room, I began to dance by myself. Olivia came running up to me and tried to rub against my ankles, looking up into my face and mewing. So I picked her up and kept on dancing. She hung over my shoulder, purring loudly, obviously enjoying herself. Now, every now and then

I'll dance to music on the radio, and she always comes and asks to be picked up. She seems to like waltzes—sweeping motions—better than rock.

Paper bag: An empty grocery bag on its side on the floor—there's hardly a cat alive that doesn't like to crawl in that. And if you scratch on the side or end with a spoon or pencil (better not use your finger), the cat will ecstatically pounce, usually poking its paw right through the paper. Or, you can poke a little hole from the outside and wiggle something through to the cat inside.

Running water: A drippy faucet may be a nuisance to us but a fascination to cats. Menelaus, for instance, will play with dripping water and try to catch it. When the drip stops, he peers up into the faucet to see where it came from and down into the drain to see where it went, and makes digging motions in the drain to try to resurrect it. If you have a cat that seems to like running water, you might leave the tap on a bit for it to play with for a while. (Just don't forget and leave the house with the water dripping or you might come home to a flood.)

Tricks: The doctor who talks to his cats also taught one of them, Oz, to roll over. He used little bits of food the cat loved as reward. To begin, he pushed the cat gently down on its side with the command, "Roll over," then rewarded it. Soon Oz learned to lie down. Then the owner rolled the cat over when he gave the command, rewarding it immediately. In this way, step by step, he got Oz to roll over on command —always for a reward, of course.

Cats have also been taught, by way of rewards and patience, to jump over barriers and perform other simple tricks. Of course, the younger the cat, the easier it is. I doubt if I could get much enthusiasm from sixteen-year-old

Fred to do tricks now. He's too sophisticated; if I tried, he would just think I'd gone a little crazy and walk away.

If you're observant, you'll notice traits in your cat that are exclusive to its own personality and that both of you enjoy. Cultivate those traits by encouraging and responding to the cat whenever it expresses them. My cat Gina, for example, learned early that we thought she was especially enchanting whenever she rolled on her back in a curl, as I described earlier, with her paws held coyly under her chin. We notice, make a fuss, pet her, tell her how cute she is. So naturally, this behavior has become an established trick in her repertory.

It is during play that a cat expresses its sense of humor—in games with you, by itself, and especially with others. One cat ambushing another is teasing the other cat, but also having a private joke. When Katie dunked the kitten's face in the food, it seemed to all of us who saw her do it that she was amusing herself at the little upstart's expense. When Menelaus' owner walks by him, sometimes he'll dart up and tap her on the foot, then tear away. He probably thinks that's the funniest thing in the world. It's hard to say that when a cat goes into a comical pose that makes you laugh, it knows it is funny—but why not? One cat I know, Sweeny Todd, sits on top of the TV when his owner has a hockey game on and watches the game upside down, batting his paw back and forth following the action. Is Sweeny really trying to catch those hockey players, or does he think it's funny to play the clown by peering upside down and trying to bat some moving objects on the screen?

People who accuse others of being anthropomorphic about their pets make a puzzling assumption. In their anthropocentrism, they presume that emotions such as love, anger, jealousy, sympathy, humor, generosity, and so forth are exclusively human and that other animals are incapable of feeling them. This point of view is a holdover from Descartes, who argued that animals are mere machines that respond to stimuli. A person who believes this today is unaware that he or she is reflecting seventeenth-century Cartesian thought, but those ideas seem to die hard. A century later, Voltaire replied to Descartes: "Answer me, machinist: has nature arranged all the means of feeling in this animal, so that it may not feel?" And in the nineteenth century, Darwin said, "Most of the more complex emotions are common to the higher animals and ourselves." Animal studies today bear out and advance this knowledge.

And yet, if I tell someone that Olivia will step aside and let Gina eat from her bowl, even though she wants the food herself, because she's generous to her friend, I meet a dubious smile. Anyone who watches animals—pet, domestic, wild, or captive—knows well that animals certainly do feel and express complex emotions, among themselves and with human beings. I can never understand why so many people are so surprised at what animals do. The highly developed emotions are, as Darwin suggested, common to all sentient vertebrates. If you feel love from your cat, it loves you.

Toys for a cat

Because its world is limited by the walls of your house or apartment, an indoor cat does need perhaps more toys than one that can go out and chase a leaf across the lawn. Enter the home of a fond cat owner and you'll find toys scattered around the floor and in odd places such as under the sofa pillows.

One woman I know was working on some kind of crafts project one evening when her cat came to investigate what she was doing. To occupy him, she gave him a large wooden bead (much too big for him to swallow), and he danced off across the floor after it in high glee. As the evening wore on, he lost it, so she gave him another, then another. Over several evenings as she worked, her cat seemed to ask for an inordinate number of large wooden beads, but she didn't think much about it because cats are always losing their spools, balls, and other rolling toys. Several weeks later, however, she happened to remove a large book from the bottom shelf of a bookcase and a bead rolled out. Putting her hand back of the volumes, she felt what turned out to be a neat little pile of about a dozen large wooden beads. The cat had carefully stashed away his treasure.

While every cat will love a ball or catnip mouse, many good cat toys are ordinary household objects:

wine cork
empty spool
old sock
twisted pipe cleaner
pencil
wad of paper (but no cellophane, foil, or plastic)
drinking straw
bottle cap
Ping-pong ball

An empty box or an open paper bag on the floor, mentioned above, is fun for a cat to play in, and even more fun for two cats. One will hide in the box or bag and ambush the other as it walks by, or the cat on the outside will sneak up on the hiding cat. Just be sure, especially if you've put down a big paper bag or box for your pets some days previously, not to forget and step on it or discard it without looking first to see who may be crouched inside it. This mistake can be made with kittens, or if there's throw-away stuff in the carton in addition to your cat.

Catnip, an herb that acts as a mild nerve stimulant, is a sure-fire turn-on for cats and makes them feel like playing and exercising. My cats roll in it in ecstasy. (Catnip was formerly believed to be an aphrodisiac, but this has proved to be untrue for both cats and people.) You can grow catnip in flowerpots for your cat. Some vets say catnip is not good for cats with kidney problems, by the way.

Cats love to think they have found toys themselves. One cat owner I know doesn't just hand a new toy to her pets—she puts it on a table or chair, or, if it's made with catnip, behind a sofa pillow. Her cats have the fun of discovery, as well as the pleasure in the toy itself.

I sometimes recycle my cats' toys, just as I did my children's when they were small. If I notice a toy lying around that they've ignored for some time, I put it away for a month or so. Then when I get it out for them, it seems new to them. They'll play with it with new enthusiasm, as if they'd never seen it before.

Toys to avoid:
   toys with rubber bands, beads, buttons, bells, strings, or
      ribbons attached
   toys small enough to be swallowed
   soft rubber toys that might be chewed up and swallowed
      in bits (hard rubber is okay)
   anything glass
   painted cloth, leather, or wooden toys

Playing with your pet is probably the most mutually rewarding activity you'll have, perhaps even more fun than snuggling. It provides opportunity for you to observe an important side of this remarkable animal—its humor, its grace, its marvelous atavistic hunting and capturing abilities. Play makes the pet itself more interesting. And in addition to havng the pleasure of stroking the tiger, you can enjoy to the fullest what this small domestic tiger is all about.

Sitting and sleeping places

One of the most fascinating aspects of cat behavior is the number of places and positions the animal can find to sit or sleep in. I'm not talking just about hiding places, such as the closet, in back of the stove, in a garment bag, or between the shower curtains on the edge of the tub—these are, of

course, terribly important to this creature. I mean also the
way they'll perch in plain view way up on shelves that hold
plants, curl up in the washbowl, and sit up tall in the middle
of a package you've just laid on the bed. I heard of a cat
that found a crawl space between a dropped ceiling and the
actual ceiling of his owner's kitchen; it liked to crouch up
there and gaze down at the top of everybody's head.

Gina has a thing about baskets. She sleeps in her own basket on the windowsill; she also sleeps part of nearly every
day in Dandy's bed, a large basket. But one of her favorites
is an elongated bread basket, which she could fit in nicely
when she was a kitten but now bulges over the sides. The
fact that she's too fat for the narrow basket doesn't deter her
a bit. She'll get all four feet in and then ease herself down
gently until she is puffed up over the sides like a big mush-
room, and then gaze at us solemnly over the tops of her eyes
while we're howling with laughter at the sight of her.

Cats do have a precise sense of space—how else do you explain my three cats lying in the exact center of each of the
three seat cushions on my sofa?

Their ability to fall asleep in remarkable places and positions is well known to every cat owner and well documented
by cat photographers, who find these animals marvelous
subjects. Cats can also find the warmest spot in any house,
especially as they get older (see Appendix, *The geriatric
cat*). I was puzzled one cold winter when Olivia took to
sleeping on the floor in a corner under a bookshelf when
there were so many more comfortable spots to sack out.
Then I realized—of course, there's a heat riser in the wall
right there.

The sociable, affectionate cat

Indoor cats are exposed to visitors and strangers far more
than indoor-outdoor cats, and while some shy cats run and
hide at the sound of the doorbell, others are right there to

investigate every person who comes in the door. Some cats are never seen by guests; they disappear at the sound of the first voice and then drift back into the room like smoke after the last visitor has departed. Others insist on being the center of attention. Extroverted cats like Ivan, for instance, come right up, stand on their hind legs, and sniff your face. Menelaus sits right where everyone is gathered and obviously expects to be included. Gina has to be lifted out of chairs so guests can sit down.

Some cats, like Olivia, warm up by degrees. She is nowhere in sight as people enter my apartment. But after they have sat around for a while, she appears, checks everyone out, and goes from lap to lap as she pleases. (For cats and visiting children, see Appendix.)

Cats who are close to their owners may be amazingly tuned in to their feelings. Some owners claim their pets try to console them when they're unhappy, and I'm sure it's true. Menelaus' owner swears her cat comes in a hurry if she's crying. On the other hand, Pushkin and Llama's owner claims her normally highly affectionate cats ignore her when she weeps. In my case, it's hard to say because, if I cry, Dandy is always right there with her paws in my lap trying to lick my face, and the cats couldn't really get very near me if they tried, simply because Dandy is so much bigger than they are. My feeling is that cats are upset when their owners are, but not all of them express it in the same way.

Cats have been known to warn their owners of danger, rouse them when there's smoke, and the like. The cat of a friend of mine was sitting on the sill of a window that looked out on to a garden one night when it suddenly began to mew agitatedly. Its owner peered out and didn't see anything, so she concluded the cat only saw a moth or some such. She went out for the evening. When she came home, the garden window had been forced open and her apartment robbed.

I don't know if cats are protective of their owners in the

way that dogs are. While my dog Dandy is about as gentle
and good-natured as they come, I think she might bark and
perhaps even bite if I were violently attacked. It's hard to
say for sure because she has never bitten anybody or anything in her life, but it's nice to think the instinct is there.
Cats would more than likely hide.

Menelaus' owner says he came to investigate and showed
great concern once when she fell down. I think that is unusual, though cats' intelligence varies from one to another as
much as that of members of other species, including ours.
Indoor cats above all others seem to take on what we call
human characteristics because they live so closely with us.
And as I said earlier, a pet cat will be as interesting as we
encourage it to be.

The owner of an indoor cat has a twofold advantage: You
have the opportunity to develop the animal's potential for
human companionship to the fullest, while at the same time
you get a close contact with a form of animal life not our
own but endlessly intriguing. An animal that, when treated
well, can live with us with perfect poise and yet give us a
glimpse of wildness—what other creature can do that? That
is why people who love and understand cats seem to do so
passionately.

Dogs are marvelous animals for totally different reasons.
It has been said that we need dogs for pets to keep our egos
up, but we need cats to keep our egos humble. That's what
has fascinated people for thousands of years, what has
caused fear of cats among the superstitious and hatred of
cats among despots. Here's a very small animal that is dependent on people, yet on its own terms. An indoor cat has
far less control over its terms—if you abuse or neglect it, it
can't just run away as an outdoor cat will. The indoor cat
strikes a different bargain with us.

"Ignore me," it seems to say, "and I'll be simply a quiet
presence in the house. But treat me well, and I will provide

you with my companionship, my intelligence, my beauty, my unique traits, and above all my love in a way that no other animal on earth can. I will fascinate, amuse, delight, and comfort you. I will return your investment a thousand times over."

appendix

Miscellaneous Information
for Indoor Cat Owners

The cat and babies and children

A cat has lived with its owners for several years, is the apple
of their eye and accustomed to lots of attention and affection. Suddenly a new baby enters the household. Will the
cat be jealous? Might it attack the baby?

I think it depends on the owners. There's no evidence that
cats regard babies as their natural enemies, and I've never
heard or read of a cat launching an attack on a baby. It's unlikely that the entry of a new baby into a household would
be resented by the cat if it feels loved and is reassured that
the baby will not replace it in the owners' affections. Also, as
the baby grows older, if the parents teach the baby how to
respect the cat, the animal will realize the baby is not a
threat. It will come to accept and love the child if the whole
situation is handled right.

If the parents like the cat and treat it well, and insist that
the baby learn to do the same, the cat gets the message and
puts up with the little kid's unintentional clumsiness. We

had a big good-natured cat named Katie when my children were little. We always intervened if either baby got a stranglehold on Katie, but she was a paragon of tolerance. Nobody ever got scratched.

In fact, you probably won't believe this, but I actually saw Katie behave in a very maternal way with my son once when he was a baby. She had calmly endured his awkward efforts at petting and holding her. One day when he was nearly two, however, he vigorously pulled her tail (not accidentally). Like a flash, her paw was on his arm, claws out just enough to prick him slightly. Startled, he didn't move, and she left her paw on his arm for maybe four seconds. He wasn't hurt or insulted enough to cry, but he got the message.

I know of a cat that was banished from a home because it scratched the toddler. Kitzel was a cat whose position in the household had never been secure in the first place—neither the husband nor the wife really loved her. No doubt the baby's arrival had been a threat to this already uneasy and unhappy cat. So one day when the baby made a grab for the cat, she reacted. The simpleminded parents believed the cat had turned dangerous, gave her away immediately, and spoke as if they were punishing a criminal. Poor Kitzel—had she been in a home with understanding owners who cared enough about her to prevent the scratch, her subsequent ouster would not have occurred.

Naturally, a cat that is truly bad tempered should not be in a home with a little child, because it would be unpredictable if the child provoked it. But a loved cat that is confident of its place in the home will usually keep out of reach of a rambunctious baby, or will manage to squirm away if grabbed and squeezed.

I once saw a baby in a household with several cats do a curious and amusing thing. He was crawling around on the floor playing with a toy when I saw him bat it just as a cat does. Swiftly he crawled after it and batted it again. The catlike motions were unmistakable. Then he picked up the toy and dropped it behind some books on the bottom shelf of the bookcase, just as cats sometimes do with their toys. I realized that this baby had probably sat in his playpen and watched the cats play with their toys, and he assumed that was how you did it.

Cats who are raised with children generally can take little kids in stride all their lives. And cats like Gina think all people, no matter how small, noisy, and active, are just swell. But cats who have lived only with adults are often afraid of children. Olivia and Fred have to be dragged, stiff with fear, from under the bed for some young child to pat. I know they would not scratch unless they panicked and were struggling to flee. If your cat is afraid of children, be very careful about handling it with a child around. It would probably never attack, but might harm you or the child in trying to get away.

One big problem cats have with children, however, is brought about by parents who acquire the pet to "teach the children to be responsible." The parents believe that bringing a dependent animal into the household will somehow magically make the children assume responsibility for it. Only parents can teach children how to be responsible. No cat should have to depend for its food and other care on a child. The parents must instruct, insist, and supervise until the child gets the knowledge and the habit. And then the parent must continue to check up to be sure that the pet is cared for properly, every day. Children, no matter how well meaning, forget.

The cat and the dog

At least half the people who come into my home for the first time express surprise that I have cats *and* a dog. "Do they get along?" they ask in wonderment.

The phrase "fighting like cats and dogs" does have some basis in truth, because domestic cats have been known to attack dogs, and some dogs do kill cats. It's curious that this is so, because in the wild, felines and canines are not enemies, do not compete, and have separate hunting preferences and territories. I suspect that when animosity exists, it has been created by human beings. Some people, even presumably adult people, think it's funny to sic dogs on cats. And some hunting breeds of dogs may confuse house cats with the small game they have been taught to kill. A cat that has had to run for its life from dogs will not take kindly to the next dog it meets, and may be waiting for the chance to attack first.

Yet in millions of households, dogs and cats cohabit at least in mutual respect and often in mutual love. My dog, Dandelion, was raised with cats who apparently convinced her very early that cats are tops, because she seems to believe this. Cats and even the smallest kittens that come into our house, or cats that she meets elsewhere, get the message very fast that she means them no harm, and they relax. Among my cats, Olivia tolerates Dandy with grudging affection, and Fred likes her okay. But Gina adores her, rubs against her affectionately; sometimes they lie on the rug almost clasped in each other's paws.

One problem with introducing a grown dog and cat to each other is that the dog, in curiosity or playfulness, may scare the cat by rushing at it. The dog means no harm at all, but the cat doesn't believe that. It helps to have the dog on a leash when it approaches the cat so it can't bounce at it. This should be continued for the first week or so. Let the cat have plenty of high places to leap to and survey the dog from, and reassure it lavishly. Exercise a lot of patience with both animals.

Best way to have a dog-and-cat combination of pets is to start with a kitten and a puppy. Give them both a lot of affection and they will most likely grow up to be good friends. If you already have a dog, however, success depends on the animal's temperament. If the dog is excitable or jealous by nature, it's best not to bring in a defenseless kitten; I would choose a good-natured, sophisticated, full-grown cat. Give the dog a great deal of extra attention while letting it know that the cat is welcome and has rights of its own. Feed them in separate rooms at first. A new kitten in my house once rushed over and stuck its head in Dandy's bowl while she was eating. Dandy's response was simply to eat faster. I removed the kitten at once, of course, but I realized that a less amiable dog might have snapped at or even bitten the cat.

If you already have a cat that's a cynical, tough dog-hater, an innocent puppy should not have to defend itself against such an animal.

Nevertheless, in general, a normal adult dog will accept a kitten and a stable adult cat will get used to a puppy eventually. Use common sense and caution. Don't force the friendship; let the two animals adjust to one another gradually. And if one human member of your family is dubious and anxious around them, and is convinced that mayhem will ensue, ask that person to stay in another room and out of the way when the two pets have their first contacts. If you are calm and confident, it will help the animals.

Traveling with a cat

I have known cats that travel all over the world with their owners with perfect poise. They were all introduced to this life-style when they were very young kittens, and seem comfortably suited to it. I've also known cats that travel with their owners back and forth to second homes, usually at the beach or in the country, and aren't bothered in the least. But, in general, most cats are homebodies, and even though they may adapt quickly and happily to a new place, getting there

—whether by car, plane, or whatever—may confuse and upset them. You can ease the trauma.

Here are a few important suggestions that apply to all modes of travel:

1. Be sure all the cat's vaccinations are currently in effect. Never travel with a cat that has recently been ill. And if you're going for an extensive stay, find out where the nearest veterinarian will be, in case of medical emergency.

2. If you're taking the cat out of the United States, make sure well in advance that you have the proper health certificates in order. Ask the consulates of the countries you'll be visiting exactly what's required (don't expect your vet to be up on the regulations of every country). Even some states vary in such requirements as rabies shots. And Hawaii has a 120-day quarantine on all incoming animals. The U. S. Travel Service, based in Washington, D.C., can give you information on domestic and foreign regulations.

3. Get your cat a collar with complete identification (your name and full address) on it to wear while traveling. If you'll be staying in one place with your cat, have *that* address and phone number on the tag. (No point in having your home address when you're someplace else with the cat!) You can get your pet permanently marked with a little tattoo, usually on the inside of its thigh, that's filed with a central agency; some lost or stolen pets have been returned through these registries. (One is I.D. Pet of Garwood, New Jersey.) Ask your veterinarian about the tattooing. But, generally, if you lose a cat in a strange place, your chances of ever seeing it again are poor. So be very careful.

4. Get your cat a good strong carrier, big enough for the animal to stand up and to stretch out in. (Some airlines insist that you buy and use their special carrier.) Make sure it has a secure latch—all you need to make a trip complete is to have the carrier fall open and spill your cat in the middle of a crowded airport or at a ferryboat dock, say, with one boat

a day that's about to depart. Unless your cat is afraid of the carrier, have the carrier out for several days before the trip so your cat can investigate it calmly. Put some of its toys in. In winter, pack a lot of thick towels or pieces of blankets around the floor and sides, to conserve the animal's body heat. But if you're traveling in summer, bear in mind that a carrier with a plastic see-through dome will overheat more quickly than other types. In fact, for summer traveling, a wire cage that permits air circulation is the most comfortable for the cat. Put two animals together in a carrier only if they're devoted friends; otherwise use separate carriers.

5. If your pet is especially nervous or timid, it might endure a trip better if it's tranquilized. Some weeks before the trip, ask your veterinarian to prescribe a tranquilizer and try it on the animal to be sure of the dosage. You don't want your animal unaffected by a too-small dose, or unconscious from an overdose. (One experienced veterinarian suggests that if the owner traveling with a pet is unduly anxious, he or she might need the tranquilizer more than the pet!) Give the cat water before and during a trip, but don't feed it for six or eight hours in advance.

By car: If possible, try getting your cat used to the car before the actual trip. Let it explore the inside of the car; put it in its carrier and take it for short trips. The idea is to help the cat realize a moving car is not a dangerous, crazy place to be.

It's not a good idea to drive with your cat walking around loose inside the car. If you have a very calm cat and someone else along to take charge of it, I suppose it wouldn't hurt to let it lie on the seat. But for its own protection, it seems to me it would be better off in its carrier, just as a baby is safer strapped into a car seat than on someone's lap.

Feed the cat only on arrival at your destination or when you stop for the night, not during the trip.

Find out in advance what motels and inns along the way

will permit cats to stay in your room, and make reservations. There's a directory, "Touring with Towser," that lists hotels and motels that accommodate guests with dogs. Such places might also allow cats. The booklet sells for $1.00; Gaines Dog Research Center, 250 North Street, White Plains, New York 10625.

Whether you're traveling across town or across the continent with your cat, do not leave it alone in a parked car. This results in one of the biggest cat killers: heat stroke. Veterinarians see many cats suffering from this condition and usually can't save them. Even in cold weather, even with the car windows open a crack, the temperature inside a car can become high enough to send a cat into heat stroke and death. And, of course, even a car parked in what is shade at ten o'clock may be in the sun at eleven. It's unsafe to leave an animal in a parked car during the day at any season, and unsafe in a parked car even at night in hot weather, period.

If you do find a cat suffering from heat stroke, there are emergency first-aid measures you can take to try to save its life, on the way to a veterinarian (see Chapter Six).

Don't yield to the impulse to let your pet out of the car to stretch its legs. That well might be the last time you'll ever see it. Somewhere in the United States, I hope in a good home, is a handsome cat named John, pure white with one blue eye and one yellow eye, who once belonged to my daughter. While waiting for her car to be repaired one summer day in a California city, she took him out of the car to a pretty little park for a breath of air. She only took her eyes off him for a moment, but that was long enough. He disappeared. She spent many hours in that neighborhood long after her car was fixed, searching for John, but to no avail.

By plane: Find out well in advance which airline goes nonstop, or makes the fewest stops, to the destination your pet will have to fly. Then get the details from that airline on its regulations—the type of carrier that's required, what health certificates are necessary, and so on. Also find out where the cat will ride on the plane—can it travel in the cabin with you? If it has to go in the baggage compartment, what are the conditions there? A cat will, of course, die in an unheated, unpressurized cargo hold. If the airline tells you the cargo compartment is heated or air-conditioned, it means it is when the plane is *in flight*. Therefore, a pet stuck in a carrier in a baggage hold during a long layover on the ground at Bismarck, North Dakota, or Miami, Florida, could die from cold or heat. And sometimes animals have survived plane trips safely, only to expire when left for a time with other baggage in the blazing sun on the runway.

These are all matters you have to consider when taking a pet by plane, unless it can ride in the cabin with you.

By train: Many railroad lines—Amtrak, for example—won't allow pets on its trains at all. This is an odd rule, isn't it, at a time when the public is being encouraged to conserve energy by using public transportation?

If you do plan to take your animal on a railroad that permits pets, try to insist that it ride in the coach or sleeper with you rather than in the baggage car. You'll want to inquire well in advance. If your cat does have to go in the baggage car, be sure to find out the conditions—whether the car is heated or air-conditioned, whether the animal will be given water and—if the trip is long—food, and whether you can visit your pet along the way. I once rode all the way from Philadelphia to Knoxville, Tennessee, mostly in the baggage car with my dog, but that was many years ago, when rules about such matters were likely to be more relaxed.

It might be a good idea to insure your pet if it's going in the baggage car. You will most certainly want to insure it if it's going by train without you.

To ship a cat: There's a company called World Wide Pet Transport that will ship your cat door-to-door to and from almost anywhere. For details, contact World Wide at 96-01 Metropolitan Avenue, Forest Hills, New York 11375.

Leaving a cat home when you travel

You're going on a trip and can't take your cat with you, or taking it along would clearly make it miserable—what's the best provision to make for it? Some cat lovers are so fazed by this question that they prefer not to own cats, fearing that if they did, they would feel tied down. It's fine to take a cat along if 1) it's used to traveling, or 2) you're going to a place the cat knows, or 3) you'll be staying somewhere long enough for the cat to recover from the trauma of the trip and become comfortable in the strange surroundings. Otherwise, the animal itself might prefer to stay home. But that doesn't mean you have to.

Lots of people leave their cat or cats completely alone for weekends, with just extra food and a clean litter box. I think this is insane—not only cruel but gambling with the animal's life. You can come home to a dead or dying cat that got sick or injured itself when there was no one to notice. You can come home to a very anxious or depressed cat, especially if you make a habit of doing this. The animal needs to know it hasn't been abandoned, even if it is perfectly safe. Some cat owners seem to treat their pets as though they were house plants that need only water and light.

There are several good options that can be satisfactory to both you and your pet. The ideal one, as far as the cat is concerned, is to have responsible friends move into your house or apartment for the duration of your absence and substitute for you in caring for it. The cat will still miss you, but it won't be lonely, and its familiar surroundings and routine will remain the same.

The next best solution is a good sitter who will come in at least twice daily. He or she should do more than just put food down and tend to the litter box—a good sitter will also talk to your animal, pet it, spend some time just being with it. The sitter should know cats well enough to recognize the classic symptoms of illness and to take the initiative to get help for your pet if necessary. He or she should have the sense to seek out the animal if it doesn't appear (apprise the sitter of the cat's hiding places), and should know your cat individually enough to spot abnormal behavior.

The sitter should be thoroughly familiar with serious cat dangers such as the high-rise syndrome or chewed material (a cat upset by its owner's absence might take on habits it didn't have before). He or she should even be understanding enough to notice if the cat's favorite toy is missing, to search for it, and get it out from under the couch or wherever.

You should leave the name, address, and telephone number of your veterinarian, and your itinerary, for the sitter, just in case of emergency. The phone number of a close friend who knows your pet is not a bad idea either.

Good sitters can be either personal friends or professionals that you hire. If you can get the same sitter regularly whenever you go away, so much the better. The main thing, however, is that it be someone you can trust absolutely with your pet.

Incidentally, if you travel a lot, this is one life-style where just out of simple kindness, you should have more than one pet. An only cat, especially a single indoor cat, really suffers when its owner is away, even with a good sitter coming in. A little animal all alone in a house or apartment, day after day, night after night, has a very anxious and lonely time. This is one of the most persuasive reasons I know of for having at least two pets.

I've known cats who are happy enough when left in "fos-

ter" homes when their owners travel. The foster home might
be simply the home of a friend of the owner, or the home of
a person who boards cats temporarily. Be cautious in choosing a foster boarding home from an advertisement. Inspect
it thoroughly yourself before you take your pet there. If the
foster home insists on a health certificate routinely from
your cat, it's a good sign. Ask for references, and check them
out. Also, find out who the veterinarian is that the foster
home uses. If the foster "parent" is really nice to animals, and
the home is a good one for a cat, this can be a satisfactory
arrangement.

But I have never known a cat that was happy at being left
in a boarding kennel. Most cats are severely upset at being
in a cage, even in a luxurious kennel. Most are severely
stressed if there are barking dogs around. If you *must* leave
your pet in a kennel, always inspect the cage and area
where it will be kept. The place should be clean and if not
quiet, certainly not bedlam. The cages should not have wire-
mesh floors—those are harmful to cats' feet. Ask if the kennel
has a veterinarian on call. If the kennel managers insist on
your leaving your animal in the reception room and are reluctant to take you behind the scenes, you don't want that
kennel. It might be perfectly okay, but you need to see for
yourself.

N.B. If you're leaving your pet anywhere but in its own
home, be sure all its inoculations are up to date.

The owner of Margot, Mistletoe, and Albert travels frequently and is blessed with a wonderful next-door neighbor
who is always willing to be the sitter for her three cats.
Whenever my friend comes back from a trip, however,
Margot lets her owner know she has been displeased by her
absence. While Mistletoe and Albert fawn all over her, uttering little mews of welcome, Margot is cool and indifferent,
will even stroll out of the room without looking at her
owner. After an hour or two, Margot apparently feels she has

made her point, and suddenly she's all over her owner, purring and following her about, leaping into her lap. Just goes to show you—even with two housemates and a doting sitter, a cat misses the person it loves, and the bond between them is strengthened and renewed each time the person returns.

The geriatric cat

Because indoor cats tend to live so long, the chances of your having a very old cat in your household are high. And like old people, elderly cats tend to have somewhat more health problems and need greater care than they did when they were young.

Cats over twelve begin to lose flesh along their backbones, and when you run your hand along their backs, you can feel the vertebrae of their spines, even when their stomachs are nice and round. They especially tend to have kidney problems. They get cataracts. Their hearing acuity diminishes. Heart disease is not uncommon. They catch cold more easily, and suffer more from heat. They need more brushing. Fatty tumors, constipation, and arthritis all afflict old cats. When he was about fourteen, Fred grew a fatty tumor on his side that gave us a scare until our vet pronounced it harmless.

You will want to keep a close eye on your elderly pet and take it to the veterinarian for regular checkups at least twice a year. You must get urine samples from the cat for the vet to run tests on. Kidney disease affects three fourths of all old cats. While it's normal and healthy for the older cat to drink more water, excessive drinking can mean kidney trouble.

Some elderly cats do better on smaller-than-usual, more frequent feedings. Baby food (meat) mixed with regular cat food seems good for an old cat's digestion. Also, you can get special geriatric-diet canned cat food through veterinarians. The old cat's diet should include cooked vegetables and a little bran if it tends to become constipated. While you shouldn't give spicy and salty foods to a cat anyway, these foods are especially harmful to an old cat. Cut down on feeding it meat and increase eggs, cottage cheese, cooked oatmeal, and rice in its diet. In fact, if you have a young cat as well as an old one, it would be a good idea to get it used to a partly vegetarian diet now as insurance for its old age.

Any persistent cough an elderly cat develops should never be ignored, nor should rapid breathing; either might be symptoms of heart trouble. In fact, slight symptoms that, in a young cat, you might consider waiting a day or so before consulting your vet about should, in your old cat, have immediate professional attention.

While nobody believes that grotesque heroic measures should be taken to keep an old cat alive if it becomes seriously and painfully sick, nevertheless there are many medications now that can keep an elderly cat comfortable and in comparatively good health for many years.

In Fred's case, he deserves the best and will get it. His devotion to me and mine to him will help him live, I hope, for years to come. And one more nice thing: As far as Gina and Olivia are concerned, and even according to visiting cats, Fred is still top cat around here.

Euthanizing a cat

A family is moving to California and for various reasons it is impossible to take their elderly cat with them. A cat owner develops a serious medical problem and can no longer take care of his or her cat. A cat owner is marrying someone who is allergic to cats. A family finds just the apartment they have been searching for—but in a building that forbids pets. A family is breaking up and nobody is in a position to cope with the pet. An elderly person is moving into a retirement or nursing home where pets are not allowed. Life circumstances do sometimes change drastically, and people do find themselves faced with having to give up a pet cat.

If you've ever been in that position, you know that it is extremely difficult to locate someone who will take your pet and give it a good home. Thanks to the people who have brought on overpopulation by allowing their cats to breed, there are more cats than homes available for them already. Virtually everybody who likes cats has cats. Sometimes you can persuade someone who has a cat or two already to take on another. Sometimes you can find that rare place, the good shelter, that will accept a healthy cat and put it up for adoption. Sometimes an advertisement you run in a newspaper will produce a good home. I adopted my beloved dog, Dandelion, seven years ago from a newspaper ad.

Some cat owners cop out with the widespread, monstrous practice of "giving it its freedom." This has a nice sound to it—freedom is a generally upbeat word—and it helps the speaker deny what he or she is really doing: abandoning a helpless animal. These people indulge in magic thinking: They kid themselves into believing that a domestic cat can survive on its own, or that someone else will come along and pick up the cat. A homeless house cat lives an average of three or four months, and its death by starvation, disease, exposure, fear, torture, or trauma is not a pretty one. A very few fortunate cats, perhaps as many as one in ten or twenty thousand, do indeed get fed or taken in by compassionate people. The rest either die or are captured and brought to pounds or shelters, where all but a few are put to death because they aren't adopted.

I remember a family of presumed cat lovers (they even had two of their own) who took in a little stray while on vacation. The cat lived with them happily and entertained the children and probably assumed its troubles were over. When the time came to go back to the city, the couple decided they wouldn't take the cat, so they simply took it to a secluded spot, tossed it out of their car, and drove quickly away.

"Oh, there was a trailer camp nearby; we're sure somebody took it in" was their magic thinking. Since children learn far more from what we do than what we say, I wonder what lesson this couple's young children got from this experience. Among other things, I guess they got the message that it's okay to dispose of a living animal as if it were a piece of Kleenex.

People who take their pet to a pound or the average shelter are at least sparing it the pain of abandonment. But they should be aware that unless the animal is an enchanting kitten, or under two years old and an extraordinary beauty, it will merely be kept for a few days in the cold comfort of a cage before it is euthanized. Some pounds kill animals by the controversial decompression chamber. The terrified animals are crowded together in a locked metal cylinder from which the oxygen is rapidly decompressed. Nobody knows if the animals suffer as they die. Some have been seen twitching, still breathing, as the bodies are shoveled out afterward.

There is also the possibility that a pet will be turned over to an experimental laboratory. In some states, public pounds and shelters are obliged by law to supply cats to medical schools and government research laboratories for experimentation; others sell animals for this purpose. So you have to consider the possibility that your pet might wind up with electrodes in its brain, its feet burned off, its stomach injected with acid, its bones broken, or enduring some other prolonged death.

A few unusual shelters neither destroy the animals they accept nor sell them to laboratories, but do take care of them until they're adopted. Some, like the Kent Animal Shelter in Calverton, Long Island, even screen potential adopters carefully and take back any animals from people who have second thoughts later. Such shelters are rare, but you might find one in your area if you had to.

One organization that offers a haven for cats whose owners can afford a modest placement fee is the National Cat Protection Society, which has a Cat Retirement-Placement Center in Spring Valley, California. There, if a cat is not adopted, it will stay and be taken care of for life. You can even send a cat and it will be met at the airport.

You might contact these places for information, or investigate to see if any organization or shelter in your area offers a good solution for pets. Naturally, you would consider only a first-rate place, run by caring and competent people.

The notion of having one's cat euthanized is a tough one for cat lovers to deal with. It is bad enough to have your pet put to death as an act of mercy when it is incurably ill and plainly suffering. Yet virtually all of us agree an animal should be accorded the *coup de grâce*—indeed, many of us would want this kindness extended to us if we were in a similar position. Nevertheless, when the time actually comes, it is very hard to make the decision, take our loved pet to the veterinarian, and hold it in our arms as its life slips away.

The idea of euthanizing in any circumstances other than incurable illness is a hundred times harder to consider. Many vets refuse to destroy a physically healthy animal. They feel they have been trained to conserve life, and killing any but an already dying or mortally suffering animal is not their job. While I can understand this attitude and respect it, it really doesn't serve the cat because of the limited number of alternatives available to an owner today who must give up a pet. The owner may be forced to take the pet to a pound or shelter where it will probably be put to death anyway, in far less humane circumstances. I believe this position on the part of some veterinarians may also increase the dumping of animals.

Euthanasia by a private veterinarian is not painful to a cat. It is not even frightening if the owner is reassuring and doesn't betray the pet by communicating his or her own distress. The owner holds the cat while the vet gives an overdose of anesthetic by injection. The cat goes peacefully to sleep. But because most of us have hangups about death, euthanasia seems horrifying to us. There may be certain extreme circumstances, however, where it is in the best interests of the cat. I believe that at such a time we all owe our pets this act of love.

I am a strong believer, by the way, in adopting a new cat as quickly as possible when one of your own has died. You can never replace the unique animal you have lost, but a new cat to love helps ease the pain of the death. I have no patience for the narrow attitude of people who claim they would never have another pet because the death of one has been so painful. I think they pretend to an exalted sensitivity. Everything worth having has its price. By avoiding one of the great anguishes of life—the loss of a pet—they also pass up one of life's most joyous satisfactions. The human heart, after all, has lots of room—you can love an unlimited number of pets, all differently.

People differ in their feelings about the disposal of the body of a pet. Suburban and country dwellers often have a nice place on their property for a pet's grave, if they wish it. City people rarely have such a spot available to them. You have a few choices: You can avail yourself of a pet cemetery or crematory (look in the Yellow Pages), or you can ask your vet or animal hospital to dispose of the body. When Baxter was terminally ill, my son finally had him euthanized by a veterinarian and paid an extra fee to have Baxter's body cremated.

When my son acquired Fidel, who looks and behaves very much like Baxter, many of his friends and neighbors didn't

realize Fidel was a different cat. He even hangs out in some
of Baxter's old haunts. It's eerie, in a nice way.

Providing for your cat if you die

People who live alone and have no close family sometimes
have a troubling thought at the back of their mind: What
would happen to their cats in the event of their own death?
You don't even have to be elderly to think of this—it can be
a worry at any age.

One quite young couple I know have included a bequest
in their will for a trusted friend to use in the care of their
two cats if they died. This is one good way to have peace of
mind about this matter. A bequest of money alone, without
any mention of who will be entrusted with the care of your
cat, is not the best solution. The court would appoint a
guardian, and decisions concerning *how* the animal will be
cared for and by whom may be made by unqualified and
indifferent people.

Remember that your pets are not automatically included
in your estate by law. You have to make specific arrangements yourself.

Another way to provide for your pets is to make an arrangement with a really fine shelter that has a specific provision for pets whose owners have died. The Kent Animal
Shelter (Calverton, Long Island) has a special Retirement
Home where, under the terms of a bequest you provide in
your will, your cat will be taken care of for the rest of its
life. It will not be put up for adoption nor live at the shelter,
but will live in a private house owned by the Kent Shelter,
with resident "parents" and a few other pets. The cat will
also get any veterinary care it ever requires.

Or, you might leave a bequest that would cover your cat's
transportation and admittance to the National Cat Protection Society's Retirement-Placement Center in Long Beach,

California. Also, there might possibly be a humane and well-run shelter in your community that offers similar arrangements for people who wish to provide for their cats.

I've instructed my son and daughter that whichever of them was lucky enough to inherit Fred, Olivia, and Gina should remember to give Fred his eye medicine, talk to Olivia, and keep Gina from pulling the box of Friskies out of the cupboard and stuffing herself between meals.

Index

Abdominal pain, 68
Abyssinian cats, 19, 20, 106
Acid and alkali poisons, 69–70
Adolescent cats
  feeding, 36
  mix and match, 24–33
Adoption, 19, 23, 106, 160, 163
  unadoptable cats, 33
Adult cats
  feeding, 35
  introducing kittens to, 24,
    27–28
  mix and match, 24–33
  vegetarian diet for old cats, 44,
    158–59
African violets, 71
Aggressiveness, 122–25
  against other cats, 125
  physical causes, 123
  stress factors, 124
Albert (cat), 29, 30, 157
Alfalfa sprouts, 43
Allergies, 95–96
Ambushing, 3, 138
Ammonia, 112
Angora cats, 19
Animal pounds, 105, 106, 107,
  161
  cats from, 21, 23
Animal shelters, 105, 106, 160,
  161, 162
Animal studies, emotions, 139
Anthropomorphism, 130, 138
Antifreeze (ethylene glycol), 69
Aphrodisiac, 140
Appetite loss, 82, 83, 84, 87, 90

Arthritis, 123, 158
Ascarids (roundworms), 89
Ascorbic acid, 40
Ash
  in cat food, 38–39
  and urinary disorders, 38–39
ASPCA, 23, 64
Aspirin, 83

Bacon fat, 39
Bad habits, how to avoid or cure,
  108–26
Baskets, 142
Bathing, 56–57
Baxter (author's cat), 36, 41, 56,
  133, 136, 163
Beads, 73
Bean curd (tofu), 43
Becky (author's cat), 8, 15, 45,
  111, 133
Behavior
  aggressiveness, 122–25
  bad habits, 108–9
  cat's point of view, 109
  confinement stress, 4–5, 6–7,
    121
  crying, 68, 121–22
  difference between instinctive
    and preventable, 109
  how to avoid or cure problems,
    108–26
  litter-box training, 53–54;
    retraining, 111–14
  modification, 54
  neurotic, 4
  nursing, 120–21

personality traits, 138
and punishment, 109, 112, 124
and scolding, 125–26
and spanking, 111
Bells, 73
Berries, 71
Biotin, 41
Birman cats, 106
Birth-control pills, 105
Bittersweet, 71
Bleach, 67, 69
Body language, 130–32
Bone meal, 97
Bones, 40, 41
Boredom
and crying, 122
and nursing, 121
as cause of sickness, 4
Brain tumors, 123
Brandy, 67, 83
Breathing
difficult, 85
hard, 68
labored, 87
rapid, 83, 159
slow, 83
Breeding, moratorium on, 106–7
Brewers' yeast, 40, 55, 92
Broken glass, 73
Brushing, 16, 49, 54–55
Burns, 74–76
Butter, 39
Buttons, 73

Cages, 4
safari, 113
Caladium, 71
Calcium, 39
Calculi
cystic, 86
urethral, 86
Cancers, 87–88, 105
Canned fish, 38
Canned food, 38
Capture, 134

Capture (game), 136
Carla (cat), 16, 32
Carriers, 151–52, 154
Carry/carrying, 136
Car travel, 152–53
Castration, 104
Cat breeders, 22, 106, 107
Cat fever. See Panleukopenia
Catless people, 11
Catnip, 116, 119, 140
Cat-owner conversation, 128–30, 132
Cat population
euthanasia, 106, 107
reproduction regulation, 107
starvation, 106
Cat registries, 21
Cat-repellent sprays, 117
Cat Retirement-Placement Center, 162, 164–65
Cat sitter, 156
Cat's point of view, 109
Cellophane, 72, 140
Charcoal, powdered activated, 70
Charles (cat), 125
Charlie (author's cat), 82
Chasing, 5, 134
Chicken giblets, 39
Children, 146–48
and kittens, 28
Choking, 73
Choosing a cat, 18–20
male or female, 17–18
single kitten, 11–13
three or more, 15–17
two kittens, 13–15, 29
Christmas cherry, 71
Clarence (cat), 16, 32
Cleansers, 69
Cleopatra (cat), 31, 123
Coat, 54–55
dull, 82, 83, 89
Coccidia, 89–90
Cod liver oil, 43
Coleus, 71

Colici (disease), 84
Collars
 flea, 90, 91–92, 93, 95
 identification, 151
Communication, between cat and
  owner, 127–30, 132
Companionship, 5, 13, 14, 15, 24
Confinement, 2
 and neutering, 80–81
 as stress factor, 4–6
Constipation, 52, 87, 96, 97, 158
Convulsions, 68
Cottage cheese, 39, 43, 159
Coughing, 68, 83, 84, 89, 90, 159
Crayons, 67, 69
Crematory, 163
Crouching, 131
Crying, 68, 121–22
Cystic calculi, 86
Cystitis (disease), 38, 86

Daffodil, 71
Danced/dancing, 136–37
Dandelion (Dandy; author's
  dog), 55, 63, 96, 142,
  143, 144, 149, 160
Dandruff, 55
Darwin, Charles, 139
Declawing, 117
 anti- and pro-arguments, 117
 postoperative complications,
  118
Decompression chambers, 161
Dehydration, 37, 83, 90, 97
Depression, 82
Dermatitis, 55
Descartes, René, 138–39
Detergents, 69
Diabetes, 110
 mellitus, 105
Diarrhea, 52, 68, 82, 84, 87, 89,
  90, 95, 96
 in kittens, 97
Dieffenbachia, 71
Diet. See Food/feeding

Digestive disorders, 95
Diseases, 84
Distemper. See Panleukopenia
Dog food, 41
Dogs, 15, 33, 37, 99
 and cats, 148–50
 and human ego, 144
Dried flower bouquets, 71
Drinking
 excessive, 38, 82
 from faucet, 38, 137
 from toilet, 37, 38
Dry food, 36, 38–39
 ash content, 38–39, 86
 guaranteed analysis, 39
Dyes, 69, 95

Ear grooming, 56, 59–60
Ear infection, 123
Ear mites, 21, 94
Ears, 83
 position of as indication of
  mood, 131
Edema, pulmonary, 76
Eggs, 39, 43, 159
 raw, 41
 white, 41, 69
 yolks, 41, 43
Ego, 144
Egyptian cat, 44
Eldridge (cat), 15–16, 123
Electric blanket, 75
Electric cord, 75–76
Emetics, 69
Emotions, 138–39
English ivy, 71
Enteritis. See Panleukopenia
Estrus (heat), 80, 102
 drug suppressing, 105
Ethylene glycol (antifreeze), 69
Excessive thirst, 38, 82
Exercise, 6
External parasites, 90–94
Eyes, 83, 84, 85, 89, 90
 expression in, 130

Eyesight, 159

Face rub, 131
Falling, 63–67
    feetfirst landing, 66
    open windows, 65, 66
    stairwells, 65
    survival myth, 65
Fat, 38, 39, 55
Fatty tumors, 159
Faucet, drinking from, 37, 137
Feline infectious enteritis. *See*
        Panleukopenia
Feline leukemia (lymphosar-
        coma), 87–88
FeLV (feline leukemia virus),
        87–88
Females, 17
    birth-control pills, 105
    breast cancer, 105
    estrus-suppressing drugs, 105
    mammary tumors, 105
    neutering (spaying), 81,
        104–5
    urolithiasis, 86
Ferns, 71
Fidel (cat), 16–17, 136, 163–164
Fish
    canned, 38
    cooked, 39
    raw, 41, 89
Flashlight, 78, 134
Flea collar, 90, 91–92, 93, 95
Fleas, 21, 57, 89, 91–93, 99
    dips, collars, sprays, powders,
        93
Foil, 72, 140
Food/feeding, 4, 34–48
    adolescents, 36
    adults, 3–5
    after surgery, 101
    allergies, 95
    appetite loss, 82, 83, 84, 87, 90
    ash content, 39, 86

baby food, 39, 158
bland diet, 95
bowls, 44–46, 96
by hand, 47, 101
canned food, 38
change in diet, 96
cottage cheese, 39, 43, 159
dry food, 36, 38–39
eggs, 39, 41, 43, 69, 159
fat, 38, 39, 55
fish, 38, 39, 41, 89
and house plants, 118
how much and how often,
    35–37
kittens, 35–36, 39, 41
meat, 39, 41, 89, 90
milk, 41–42, 43, 69
mineral content, 39
moist (semidry), 40
no-no's, 41, 90
and obesity, 4, 6, 34–35
old cats, 44, 158–59
problems, 46–48
protein, 38, 39, 43
refusal to eat, 47
snacks, 36
storing unfinished food, 37
temperature, 41
vegetables, 39, 40, 42–44, 159
vitamins, 38, 40, 41, 43, 92
and vomiting, 47–48
Footpads, 83
    burn on, 74–75
Foreign objects, swallowing,
    71–73
Foster homes, 157
Fred (author's cat), 11, 14, 15,
    18, 19, 32, 38, 42, 48, 55,
    59, 65–66, 77, 81, 115,
    116, 124, 125, 132, 134,
    135, 137–38, 149, 158,
    159, 165
Furniture clawing, 6, 109,
    114–16

FVRCP (Feline Virus Rhino-
    tracheitis Colici Panleuko-
    penia) vaccine, 84–85

Gaines Dog Research Center,
    153
Games, 132–39
Gasoline, 69
Gina (author's cat), 11, 15, 28,
    32, 42, 48, 55, 58, 59, 72,
    115, 116, 132, 133, 138,
    139, 142, 149, 159, 165
Giving up a cat, 23, 106, 107,
    125, 159–64
Glass, broken, 73
Grooming, 9, 49, 54–55, 62, 87
Gums, 61–62
    pale, 83, 87

Hair balls, 96, 97–98
Hand-feeding, 47, 101
Hawaii
    animal quarantine, 151
    Panaewa rain forest zoo, 5
Health, 80
Health certificate, 151, 154
Hearing, 159
Heart trouble, 98, 159
Heat (estrus), 80, 102, 105
Heating pad, 75
Heat stroke, 73–74, 153
Hide-and-seek (game), 135
Hiding, 5, 6, 9, 76–79, 82, 83,
    141
High-rise syndrome, 63–67
Holly, 71
Hookworms, 89
Hormones, 105
Hotels, 153
House plants, 6, 70–71
    cats urinating in soil, 113
    eating, 118–19
    grown in bird cages, 119
    spraying, 119
Humane societies, 21

Humor, sense of, 122, 138
Hunting, 9
Hydrogen peroxide, as emetic, 69
Hygiene, 49

Identification
    collar, 151
    tattoo, 151
I.D. Pet, 151
Illness, 4
    care during, 101–2
    symptoms, 56, 81–83
Inactivity, and urinary disorders,
    38
Indoor living, adapting to, 6, 7
Insecticides, 57, 67, 69
Internal injuries, 67
Internal parasites (worms), 21,
    88–90
Invasion of territory, 25–26
Ipecac, syrup of, 69, 70
Iron, 39
Irons, steam, 74
IU vitamin capsules, 43
Ivan (cat), 126, 143
Ivy
    English, 71
    Swedish, 71

Jealousy, 25, 126
John (cat), 153

Kaopectate, 97
Katie (author's cat), 25, 28, 45,
    138, 147
Kelp, 43
Kennels, 157
Kent Animal Shelter, 161–62,
    164
Kerosene, 69
Kidney disease, 110, 140, 158
Kipling, Rudyard, 3
Kismet (cat), 90
Kittening, moratorium on, 106
Kitten mills, 22, 106

Kittens, 25, 27–28
  and children, 28
  diarrhea in, 97
  electric cord chewing, 75
  feeding, 35–36, 39, 41
  FVRCP shots, 84–85
  getting rid of fleas, 93
  introduction to older cats, 24,
    27–28
  litter-box training, 53–54
  mix and match, 24–33
  nursing, 120–21
  playing with, 133–34
  pneumonitis shots, 85
  poison susceptibility, 67
  refusal to eat, 47
  scratching-post training, 115,
    116
  three or more, 15–17
  trained to leash, 7
  two, 13–15, 29
Kitty litter. See Litter
Kitzel (cat), 147

Laurel leaves, 71
Lentil sprouts, 43
Lethargy, 82, 89
Leukemia, feline, 87–88
Lice, 93
Life expectancy, 80
Linda (cat), 102, 110
Liquids, administering, 100
Litter, 95
  changing to different type, 111
  clay, 51
  organic pellets, 51
Litter box, 16, 49–53
  liners, 51
Litter-box training, 53–54
  breaking, 52, 86, 109, 110–14
  retraining, 111–14
Llama (cat), 31–32, 43
Loneliness, 14
Love bites, 124

Lye, 69
Lymphosarcoma (feline leuke-
    mia), 87–88

Magnesia, milk of, 69, 97
Males, 17
  neutered, 38, 103, 104
  and urolithiasis, 86–87
Malnutrition, 4
Mammary tumors, 105
Mange, sarcoptic, 93–94
Margot (cat), 29–30, 157
Mary Jane (cat), 126
Meat
  cooked, 39
  organic, 39
  raw, 41, 89, 90
Medical schools, 161
Medicine, 67, 69, 95
  administering, 99–100
Menelaus (cat), 47, 115, 134,
    135, 137, 138, 143, 144
Milk, 41–42, 43
  as emetic, 69
Milk of magnesia, 69, 97
Minerals, 39
Miracle of birth, 104
Miracle of death, 104
Mistletoe, 71
Mistletoe (cat), 29–30, 67, 157
Mites, 93
  ear, 21, 94
Mix and match, 24–33
  returning kittens when it
    doesn't work, 31, 33
  unadoptable animals, 33
Moist (semidry) food, 40
Motels, 153
Mothballs, 112, 119
Mouth, 60–61, 83, 84
  checkup, 62
Mouth-to-mouth resuscitation, 76
Mung bean sprouts, 43
Mustard, as emetic, 69

Nail clipping, 49, 57–59, 114,
    116
National Cat Protection Society,
    162, 164–65
Needles, 28, 72
Neutering, 80–81, 101–6
Nonacid and nonalkali poisons,
    68–69
Nose, 84, 85, 90
Nursing, 120–21

Oatmeal, 159
Obesity, 4, 6, 34–35
  and urinary disorders, 38
Old cats, 142, 158–59
Olivia (author's cat), 11, 17, 21,
    32, 41–42, 46, 48, 55, 59,
    78, 96, 115, 116, 128,
    132, 136–37, 139, 142,
    143, 149, 159, 165
Only cat, 13–15, 18, 156
Outdoors, indoor cats' reaction
    to, 7–9
Ovaries, removal of, 105
Ovariohysterectomy (spaying),
    105
Overeating, 82
Owner-cat conversation, 128–30,
    132
Oz (cat), 137

Paint, 57, 67, 69
Paint remover, 69
Paint thinner, 69
Palms, 71
Panaewa rain forest zoo, 5
Panleukopenia (distemper, cat
    fever, feline infectious en-
    teritis), 84
Paper bag, 137
Paper wad, 135–36
Parasites
  external, 90–94
  internal (worms), 88–90

Patient care, 101–2
Peanut oil, 43
Pecking order, 125
Pelvic structure, 64–65
Persian cats, 19, 23, 54, 92
Personality traits, 6, 138
Pet cemetery, 163
Pet overpopulation, 23, 106, 107
Petromalt, 55, 97
Pet shops, 21, 22
Petting, cats' invitation to, 132
Philodendron, 71
Phoebe (cat), 133
Phosphorus, 39
Pills, administering, 99–100
Pipe cleaner, 136, 140
Plane travel, 153–54
Plant sprayer, 112, 116
Plastic, 140
Playing, 6, 9, 132–39
Pneumonia, 84
Pneumonitis, 85
Poinsettia, 71
Poisons/poisoning, 57, 67–70
  acid and alkali, 69–70
  house plants, 70–71
  nonacid and nonalkali, 68–69
  symptoms, 68
Polishes, 57, 67, 69
Potted plants. See House plants
Pounce (game), 134–35
Pouncing, 3, 6
Pounds, 105, 106, 107, 161
  cats from, 21, 23
Pregnancy, 80
Princess (cat), 46
Protein, 38, 39
  animal, 43
  vegetables, 43
Pulmonary edema, 76
Punishment, 109, 112, 124
Puppy mills, 22
Pushkin (cat), 11–13, 31–32,
    118–19, 120, 143

Quarantine, 151

Rabies vaccination, 85–86, 151
Rat killers, 67, 69
Refusal to eat, 47
Regurgitating apparatus, 68
Reproduction, regulation of, 107
Research laboratories, 161
Respiratory disorders, 21, 95
Retrieve (game), 135
Rhinotracheitis (disease), 84
Ribbon, 72
Rice, 159
Ringworm, 94–95, 99
Roach killers, 67
Rosebud (cat), 31
Roundworms (ascarids), 89
Rubber bands, 72
Rug clawing, 116
Running water, 137

Safari cage, 113
Safety, 63
Salivation, 68
Salomé (cat), 60
Salt, as emetic, 69
Sarcoptic mange, 93–94
Scolding, 125–26
Scratching post, 114–16
Semidry (moist) food, 40
Sense of humor, 122, 138
Shelters, 105, 106, 160, 161, 162
Shipping, 154
Shock, 67, 75, 76
Siamese cats, 20, 23, 106
Sick cat, care of, 101–2
Sitting places, 9, 116, 141–42
Skin disorders, 95
Skinner, B. F., 54
Sleep, sleeping, 3, 9, 132–33,
    141–42
Sleeping places, 141–42
Smoke inhalation, 76
Soy beans, 43
Spanking, 111

Spaying, 81, 104–5
Spider plant, 71
Spraying, 80, 103
Sprays, cat-repellent, 117
Sprouts, 43
Stalking, 3, 5, 134
Steam iron, 74
Steatitis (disease), 38
Stray cats, 20–21
Stress, 4–6, 87
    and neutering, 81
    and nursing, 121
String, 28, 72
Swallowing foreign objects,
    71–73
Swedish ivy, 71
Sweeny Todd (cat), 138
Symptoms
    elderly cats, 159
    of illness, 81–83
    of poisoning, 68
Syrup of ipecac, 69, 70

Tabasco sauce, 119
Table scraps, 40
Tail, 83, 132
Tapeworms, 89, 91, 93
Tattoo identification, 151
Teasing, 138
Teeth/tooth care, 60–62, 123
Temperature, 81–82, 83, 101
    how to take, 100–1
Temperature, food, 41
Territory, invasion of, 25–26
Thirst, excessive, 38, 82
Thompson Jones (cat), 16, 32,
    91
Thread, 72
Three cats, 15–17
Throat, 84
Ticks, 93
Tinsel, 28, 71–72
Tobacco, 95
Tofu (bean curd), 43
Toilet, drinking from, 37

Tongue, pale, 83
Tonsillitis, 48
"Touring with Towser" directory, 153
Toxoplasmosis, 90
Toys, 6, 139–41
  recycling, 141
  retrieving, 135
  to be avoided, 141
Train travel, 154–55
Tranquilizers, 152
Traveling
  leaving cat at home, 155–58
  with cat, 150–55
Trembling, 68, 83
Tricks, 137–39
Tumors
  brain, 123
  fatty, 159
  mammary, 105
TV, 138
Two cats, 13–15, 29

Unadoptable cats, 33
Urethral calculi, 86
Urination, 82, 83
Urolithiasis (urinary disorders), 38, 39, 52, 86–87, 110
  stages of, 87
U. S. Travel Service, 151
Uterus, removal of, 105

Vaccinations, 80, 84–86, 151, 157
Vegetables, 39, 40, 42–44, 159
Velvet (cat), 31
Veterinarian, 21, 47, 48, 52, 59, 65, 68, 69, 72, 81, 83, 89, 91, 93, 94, 95, 102, 117, 152, 158, 159, 162
Vinegar, 112, 119
Viruses, 84, 87
Visitors, 142–43
Vitamin A, 43

Vitamin B, 41, 43
Vitamin B$_1$, 41, 92
Vitamin C, 40
Vitamin E, 43
  deficiency, 38
Vitamins/vitamin tablets, 40
Voltaire, 139
Vomiting, 47–48, 81, 82, 84, 87, 95
  as symptom of poisoning, 68
  induced (for poison elimination), 68–69

Walking, 131
Warmth, 5, 142
Washing, failure to, 56
Water, 37–38
  excessive drinking, 38
  running, 137
Water pistol, 112, 116
Wax, 69
Weight loss, 87
Wheat germ, 39, 43
Wheat germ oil, 39, 43, 55
Wheat sprouts, 43
Where to get a cat, 20–22
Whiskers (cat), 35
Whiskey, 83
White petroleum jelly, 97
Whole grains, 43
Wills, pet care provisions in, 164–65
Window screens, 6, 66
World Wide Pet Transport, 155
Worm medicines, 89
Worms, 21, 88–90

Yogurt, 39, 43

Zinc, 43
Zoo animals, 134
  and confinement stress, 4–5
  nursing, 121